NICOLE

The unofficial and unauthorised biography of
NICOLE KIDMAN
by Victoria Chow

Published by
Kandour Ltd
1-3 Colebrook Place
London N1 8HZ

This edition printed in 2004 for
Bookmart Limited
Registered Number 2372865
Trading as Bookmart Ltd
Blaby Road
Wigston
Leicester LE18 4SE

First published June 2004

ISBN 1–904756–09–3

Production services:
Metro Media Ltd

Author: Victoria Chow

With thanks to: Jenny Ross, Emma Hayley,
Lee Coventry, Belinda Weber

Cover design: Mike Lomax
Cover Image: Rex Features

Inside images: Rex Features

© Kandour Ltd

Printed and bound by Nørhaven Paperback, Denmark

NICOLE KIDMAN

FOREWORD

This series of biographies is a celebration of celebrity. It features some of the world's greatest modern-day icons including movie stars, soap personalities, pop idols, comedians and sporting heroes. Each biography examines their struggles, their family background, their rise to stardom and in some cases their struggle to stay there. The books aim to shed some light on what makes a star. Why do some people succeed when others fail?

Written in a light-hearted and lively way, and coupled with the most up-to-date details on the world's favourite heroes and heroines, this series is an entertaining read for anyone interested in the world of celebrity. Discover all about their career highlights – what was the defining moment to propel them into superstardom? No story about fame is without its ups and downs. We reveal the emotional rollercoaster ride that many of these stars have been on to stay at the top. Read all about your most adored personalities in these riveting books.

NICOLE KIDMAN

CONTENTS

NICOLE KIDMAN

FACT FILE

Full name: Nicole Mary Kidman
Eye colour: Blue
Date of birth: 20 June 1967
Place of birth: Honolulu, Hawaii
Height: 5'10$^{1/2}$"
Daughter: Isabella Jane (adopted),
born 22 December 1992
Son: Conor Antony (adopted),
born 17 January 1995
Marriage: Tom Cruise
(24 December 1990 – 8 August 2001)

Star sign: Gemini
Those of this air sign are chatty and easy to talk to,
as well as extremely amusing company. They are
curious, and have the ability to see both sides of an
argument.

NICOLE KIDMAN

FACT FILE

Chinese birth sign: Goat

While they are sensitive, artistic, creative souls, goats are true survivors who do not know the meaning of quitting. However, their feelings are also easily hurt. They like to look good and can sometimes come across as vain.

Career highlight to date:

Winning the Best Actress Oscar, the Best Actress Bafta and the Golden Globe for Best Actress in a Drama for her role in *The Hours* proved to everyone that Nicole Kidman was an actress to be reckoned with.

NICOLE KIDMAN

Nicole was born in Honolulu, Hawaii where her Australian parents, Janelle and Antony, were working. She therefore has an Australian-American passport.

Nicole has a passion for extreme activities, which has included going around a race-track at 180 miles per hour, swimming with stingrays and moray eels and skydiving.

Nicole has said that her and Tom Cruise had their first kiss – their first as themselves rather than performing before the cameras that is – during a parachute jump.

1

Introduction

NICOLE KIDMAN

INTRODUCTION

T he Academy Awards 2003. The audience was silent in the Kodak Theatre on the evening of 23 March 2003, watching Denzel Washington – the previous year's best actor recipient – open the envelope to reveal the winner of the Best Actress Oscar.

"And the Oscar goes to," he started, "by a nose..."

He did not need to finish his sentence, the audience had already started clapping and cheering for Nicole Kidman, whose role as Virginia Woolf in *The Hours* had her famously donning a prosthetic nose. Her speech, when she accepted her award, would tell Hollywood a lot about this girl, raised in

NICOLE KIDMAN

INTRODUCTION

Australia, who had finally made it all the way to the top. Teary-eyed, she made her way up to the stage.

"Thank you so much. Yes. Now I have to think. David Hare, I need your words. I have such appreciation and gratitude for this. Russell Crowe said, 'Don't cry if you get up there,' and now I'm crying. Sorry."

Russell Crowe had won the Best Actor Oscar in 2001 for his performance in *Gladiator*. Although there have often been rumours about Kidman and Crowe in the press, speculating over the nature of their relationship, they are simply very good friends who have known each other since the early Eighties, when they met through Sydney's amateur theatre scene. In March 2004 both were honoured as 'living treasures' by the National Trust of Australia – despite the fact that Nicole was born in Hawaii, and Crowe in New Zealand.

Prior to *The Hours*, Nicole had been Oscar-nominated the previous year for *Moulin Rouge!*

David Hare, the scriptwriter for *The Hours* was thanked twice by the actress in her very emotional speech. Although Nicole – heralded in the press as the first Australian actress ever to win the Best Actress Academy Award, despite the fact of her Hawaii birth – was crying almost from the

NICOLE KIDMAN

INTRODUCTION

outset, she managed to remain clear throughout.

She thanked her manager and agents, praising them for their support and career guidance.

Since *The Hours*, Nicole has appeared in *Cold Mountain*, *The Human Stain* and *Dogville* in 2003 and has made *The Interpreter*, *The Stepford Wives* and *Birth* for release in 2004. Frequently labelled 'Hollywood's hardest working actress', Nicole still manages to appear in projects and roles that suit her and do well at the box office.

The Hours is a remarkable film. Co-starring Julianne Moore and Meryl Streep – and with a supporting cast that includes Ed Harris, John C Reilly, Claire Danes and Toni Collette – it features three overlapping stories and garnered a remarkable nine Oscar nominations. It also won the Golden Globe for Best Motion Picture (Drama), and was nominated for four SAG Awards, six Golden Globes and 11 BAFTA Awards. Nicole Kidman received both the BAFTA and the Golden Globe for Best Actress for her portrayal of English author Virginia Woolf.

Based on a novel by Michael Cunningham, *The Hours* features three women who are all linked by themes of suicide and Woolf's novel *Mrs Dalloway*. We see Woolf writing the novel; Laura

NICOLE KIDMAN

INTRODUCTION

Brown (Julianne Moore) reading it in the Fifties, while struggling with her role as wife and mother; and Clarissa Vaughan (Meryl Streep) as a modern-day Mrs Dalloway, trying to organise a party to cover her empty life. *The Hours* – the original working title for Woolf's *Mrs Dalloway* – is an intelligent, well-paced film which avoids becoming over-burdened with issues, while dealing with some serious themes.

For the role Nicole, naturally left-handed, learnt to write right-handed. This is not unusual, for, as an actress, Nicole, frequently acquires new skills to aid her in her portrayals. She has learnt to swing on a trapeze for *Moulin Rouge!*, worn heavy iron shackles for *Dogville* and studied several languages and accents for roles. She has not shied away from playing dislikable characters, and does not depend on her glamour to carry a film, as her make-up work for *The Hours* proves.

The Academy Awards of 2003 were presented under the shadow of America and Britain's war in Iraq. Increased security meant that there was no red carpet area where the fans could watch the stars preening for the cameras. The sombre tone of the evening was also reflected in many of the dresses worn. Nicole herself wore black, a three-

INTRODUCTION

strap, draped and twisted gown designed by Jean Paul Gaultier that flattered her unusual beauty while sticking to the evening's sombre mood.

Many Oscar fashion commentators said that Nicole had got it right again and perhaps it was this dress that helped Nicole win the 2003 Fashion Icon Award, presented by The Council of Fashion Designers America (CFDA). Peter Arnold, executive director of the CFDA said at the time: "Nicole Kidman's style, both on- and off-screen, has had an undeniable impact on fashion... she has elegantly established her personal style and own iconic presence."

Nicole's mother, Janelle, who attended the ceremony together with Nicole's daughter, Isabella, has always been a very strong force in her life. Having survived breast cancer in 1985, Janelle has encouraged and inspired Nicole, as well as instilling strong feminist values in her.

Although Nicole's parents did not approve when she dropped out of school to pursue her acting career before getting her diploma, they have nevertheless been fully supportive of her throughout her career, and as a family, hers is very close. Janelle previously worked as a nursing instructor, while Nicole's father, Antony, is a

INTRODUCTION

biochemist and clinical psychologist, who has done extensive research into breast cancer. Her younger sister Antonia is a presenter on Australian television.

Nicole's daughter, Isabella Jane Kidman Cruise – known as Bella –was adopted by Nicole and her then husband Tom Cruise in 1993. Nicole married Cruise in 1990, at the age of 23, after they met on the set of the movie *Days of Thunder*. For more than 10 years they were Hollywood's golden couple – adopting Isabella in 1993, then a son, Conor, in 1995. Their divorce in 2001 sent shockwaves around the world. The couple – who were estimated to be worth £125 million at that time – had recently been voted the celebrity couple who set the best example of wedded bliss by readers of *New Weddings* magazine.

Despite the famous couples' infamous divorce, Cruise was one of the first people to congratulate his ex-wife on her Oscar win.

Nicole Kidman joined the upper echelons of Hollywood royalty that night. She had certainly come a long way from the 'girlfriend' roles she played when she first arrived in Hollywood – in films such as *Billy Bathgate* and *Batman Forever* – although even then she managed to inject her

INTRODUCTION

'pretty girl' roles with an edge that marked her out as different. Although she stood dutifully behind her husband in 1993 when he was given his star on the Hollywood Walk of Fame, Nicole got a star of her own 10 years later, in 2003.

When Channel 4 held a viewers' poll to discover the top 100 movie stars, Nicole was voted in at number 21. Not only was this higher than Marlon Brando, Elizabeth Taylor, Charlie Chaplin, Katharine Hepburn and Marilyn Monroe, but she also beat her ex-husband Tom Cruise (number 32) and friend Russell Crowe (number 26). The only women placed higher than her were Sigourney Weaver and Audrey Hepburn.

Yet, despite her success, Nicole continues to work harder than the majority of other actresses. While most performers of her fame and earning power make one film a year, Nicole had three films released in 2003 – *Dogville*, *The Human Stain* and *Cold Mountain* – and another two planned for release in 2004. Nor does Nicole limit herself to blockbuster movies made for big studios, preferring to take roles that will test her abilities and stretch her creatively.

Nicole's CV is a mix of comedy and drama, with a musical and a horror film varying her style

INTRODUCTION

still further. From early roles on television in Australia to starring roles in Hollywood classics, Nicole has done it all.

Not only does Nicole Kidman have stunning good looks and great pulling power at the box office, she also has artistic credibility. Nicole has earned the respect of her colleagues, working hard and turning in moving performances from a very early age. Although she dropped out of school at 16, no one doubts the intelligence and passion behind the fiery redhead's acting career, which includes television and stage work, as well as her films.

2

Starting out
Down Under

NICOLE KIDMAN

STARTING OUT DOWN UNDER

Nicole Mary Kidman entered the world on 20 June 1967. She was born in Honolulu, Hawaii where her Australian parents, Janelle and Antony, were working. This gave the young child an early advantage, an Australian-American passport, although few could have predicted quite how useful that would turn out to be in the years to come.

Soon after her birth, Nicole's parents moved to Washington, where they spent the next three years. When Nicole was three-years-old, her sister Antonia was born, and a year later the entire Kidman clan was on their way back to Sydney, Australia.

STARTING OUT DOWN UNDER

So, already there were unusual aspects to young Nicole's life, and there were to be plenty more. Nicole's parents were free-thinkers who discussed politics around the family dining table, and encouraged their daughters to be independent. Janelle was also a strong believer in feminism, and brought her daughters up to believe in their own power.

"I've never been intimidated by a man," Nicole would later say. "I never thought that because I was a woman I wouldn't be able to achieve something."

There were certainly times when Nicole rebelled against the rules, such as the Christmas when she asked for a Barbie doll. Janelle refused to buy her one, saying that Barbie was a sexist toy, Nicole went straight out and got one for herself. However, despite these minor rebellions, Nicole grew up grateful for the values her mother instilled in her, believing that the emphasis is on sisterhood, with women helping each other, because my mother always said it was about helping other women.

Nicole's father, Antony, remembers that his eldest daughter had always wanted to be an actress, and Nicole was certainly a performer at

STARTING OUT DOWN UNDER

heart from an early age. She remembers that in her first stage role – as the innkeeper's wife in the Nativity – she said everyone else's lines as well as her own. Taller than her peers from an early age, Nicole's height cost her the role of *Annie* at school when she towered over the actor who was to play Daddy Warbucks. However, the performer inside Nicole could not be contained, and she made an impressive showing the following year in the Nativity play. Cast as a sheep, Nicole's part was presumably intended to be both a small and a silent one. However, dressed in a costume Janelle made from an old sheepskin car seat, Nicole was determined to have her moment in the spotlight.

She later recalled: "When Mary was rocking the baby Jesus, I went 'Baaaaa, baaaaa, baaaaa' and of course everyone was in hysterics! This stupid kid trying to upstage Jesus as a sheep!" Although she liked people paying attention when she was performing, Nicole lacked confidence in herself when she was not on the stage. However, in retrospect, she believes that growing up with her unconventional looks made her a stronger person. "It's character-building not be a pretty child," she has said.

As she aged, Nicole saw one advantage to her

height, and that was that she had the ideal build for a ballet dancer. She began taking lessons, which would one day stand her in good stead when it came to making the musical *Moulin Rouge!*, as would a brief teenage stint as a singer in a rock band called Divine Madness. There was also a brief attempt at a modelling career which put the young Nicole on the cover of *Dolly* magazine. However, the acting side of performing kept pulling at Nicole until she gave into the temptation and joined the amateur Phillip Street Theatre group.

At this point Nicole was still very negative about her looks – and her appeal to the opposite sex. Certainly compared to the blonde-haired surfer girls, or the dark beauties like her sister Antonia, Nicole's pale skin and frizzy red hair, coupled with her height, definitely made her stand out in a crowd. Nicole would later say that her sister "has brown skin and beautiful brown hair, and I was always the one who needed to have a personality. We'd walk down the street and people would go, 'Oh, Nicole, isn't your sister gorgeous?'" This was probably the last thing Nicole needed to hear, for while Antonia was "gorgeous", she was nicknamed Stalky.

But salvation was at hand, and Nicole threw

STARTING OUT DOWN UNDER

herself into the world of the Phillip Street Theatre, spending weekends there. It provided Nicole with her first kiss when she performed in a Phillip Street production of Frank Wedekind's *Spring Awakening*. She depicted much more than a kiss, however, in her role as a sexually repressed 50-year-old Victorian, who had to yell "Beat me! Harder! Harder! Harder!" every night. When asked what her parents had thought of their 14-year-old daughter performing in such a manner, Nicole replied that they were away on holiday, but that her grandmother had really liked it.

Another who saw Nicole performing at Phillip Street Theatre was Jane Campion, who was later to be Nicole's director for *The Portrait of a Lady*. Back then Campion was a student director who wanted Nicole to appear in her graduation film, *A Girl's Own Story*. Nicole had to turn down the role when her headmistress told her it was out of the question. Campion then wrote a note to the young actress, telling her to "protect your talent".

"I hope that one day we will work together," the note read. "Be careful with what you do because you have real potential." Although Nicole had also been considering a career in journalism, she decided at this point to give acting a real try, encouraged by the reaction she was getting so far. She became a member of the Australian Theatre for Young People (ATYP), where she met like-minded individuals and learnt the skills of her trade. Years later she was to donate $100,000 to the ATYP in gratitude.

Talent-spotted at the Phillip Street Theatre, Nicole's film debut was in *Bush Christmas* when she was still only 14-years-old. The film is a remake of a 1947 film, and features the theft and recovery of a prize racehorse, Prince, who is saved by a group of children after they have braved the bush, fallen into an abandoned mineshaft and eaten bugs. Also known as *Prince and the Great Race*, this was classic children's fare which became a Christmas TV staple in Australia and held a great debut role for Nicole as one of the children on the adventure.

However, the fact she was making a film was less exciting to the 14-year-old Nicole than the fact she was not staying at home. She was expected to behave as, and was treated like, an adult, which made the experience all the more exciting. As filming ended Nicole acquired her first agent – June Caan of June Caan Management. Her professional career had truly begun.

STARTING OUT DOWN UNDER

Her next movie was *BMX Bandits*, also known as *Shortwave*, which once again concerned a group of kids foiling a criminal plot. Once again, Nicole was the lone female. She was extremely relieved that the director, Brian Trenchard-Smith, saw her character Judy as a tough girl, who could hold her own with the boys, played by Angelo D'Angelo and James Lugton.

"She is very independent and stands up for herself," said Nicole of Judy during promotion of the movie. "I think Judy is a good example to girls because she is the boys' equal and just as involved in the action as they are. She is also a terrific BMX rider and they really admire her for that."

Chase Through the Night was another crime drama, but this time it took the form of a six-part mini-series based on Max Fatchen's book. The story involved three bank robbers taking over a small town. The series was made by Howard Rubie, who had also recommended Nicole for the role in *Bush Christmas*. He said of the young actress at this time that, perhaps because of her height, Nicole seemed to feel very at ease in the company of the older actors.

Not only was Nicole seeking out adult company, she was also playing the more adult role of love interest opposite actor Brett Climo. However, she still had to study with a tutor on set, swotting up on *Romeo and Juliet* when she was not on camera.

Next on the agenda for Nicole – aside from a brief appearance in the pop video for Pat Wilson's single *Bop Girl* – was an episode of *Winners*, a television series tackling social issues affecting teenagers. The director was John Duigan who, while pleased with Nicole's performance in the episode *Room to Move*, was not so impressed with her appearance. Well, with one aspect of her appearance to be precise. Nicole later admitted that Duigan hated her wild, curly red hair, telling her that it distracted from both her face and her performance.

Despite Duigan's reaction to her hair, more modelling followed, with some work for Clairol Glints hair products. She auditioned to model swimwear as well, and although she did not get the job, she did meet someone who was to become one of her closest friends, Naomi Watts. Watts is also a movie actress, with roles in *Ned Kelly*, *The Ring*, *21 Grams* and *Mulholland Drive*, among others. When Watts won a *Movieline Magazine* Award for Breakthrough of the Year in 2001, it was a very proud Nicole who presented her friend with the prize.

By this time Nicole had grown into her looks, and was now stunning and sleek – with newly straightened and controlled hair. No one would be calling her Stalky at school any more. In fact, Nicole was not at school too often, she worked a lot and was receiving her tutoring on the set rather than in the classroom. A short TV film, *Matthew & Son* was next on the 1984 agenda, quickly followed by a brief appearance in the *Repairing the Damage* episode of *A Country Practice*.

Nicole's next film was *Burke and Wills*, a tale about two Australian heroes – William John Wills and Robert O'Hara Burke – presented in a way that makes them appear rather more foolish than heroic. Nicole's role was again as the love interest, Julia Matthews, who was adored by Burke yet ignored him throughout. Sadly another film about the duo, called *Burke and Wills*, came out around the same time. Audiences preferred the heroic epic to the comedy, but this did not prevent Nicole tackling the publicity for *Burke and Wills* wholeheartedly with great poise and professionalism.

When the offer of another job – a Disney television series called *Five Mile Creek* – was put to Nicole, she bravely broached the subject of leaving school with her parents. Nicole felt that she was already embarking on her chosen career, and that more months of school would be a waste of her time. Janelle and Antony agreed and Nicole left North Sydney High shortly before her 17th birthday. She has since commented that without her parents' support and encouragement she could not have made that decision.

Janelle later admitted that it was not easy for her and her husband to support their ambitious daughter at this time. They had hoped Nicole would go to university, but could see that she had different ideas. Although worried that acting might not provide a secure future for their daughter, they supported her wholeheartedly in her choice.

Five Mile Creek was set in the late 19th century when gold prospectors surged across Australia. Nicole was in the series for 11 episodes in 1984 playing Annie. Away on location, Nicole lived alone in Melbourne and enjoyed the attention that being in a Disney production brought professionally. Photographed by Lord Lichfield, Nicole was featured as one of Australia's 10 most beautiful women in *Harper's Bazaar* at the tender age of 17. However, she remained down to earth about her looks, and has said "I wouldn't say I was beautiful or glamourous. I would say I have a versatile face. That might be flattering myself, but it is one of my greatest assets."

Nicole was now a beautiful and attractive young woman. At the age of 17 she went to Amsterdam with a boyfriend. Although later dismissing the trip, which stretched around Europe, as "a huge mistake", while in Holland Nicole found an antique brocaded gown from the Thirties. "I thought I was going to marry the man I was with. And I didn't... But I knew it was the dress for me," she said. This, she described as a "very simple but very beautiful dress" and was the one she would wear in 1990 to marry Tom Cruise.

Upon Nicole's arrival back in Australia, she was faced with some bad news. Janelle had discovered a lump in her breast and had been diagnosed with breast cancer. Nicole moved back home and stopped working, enrolling on a massage course so she could help with her mother's physiotherapy. "It was a year in hell," Nicole said later in an interview. "She had a lumpectomy, which was new at the time, then chemotherapy and radiation. We thought she was going to die."

NICOLE KIDMAN

STARTING OUT DOWN UNDER

Nicole was not the only one to look back at this terrible time as a significant one in all the Kidman family's lives. Her sister Antonia – who was 15 at the time – admitted that the experience changed her and that she became less self-indulgent as a result. Antony would also change the focus of his career. Ten years before Janelle was taken ill he had set up the Health Psychology Unit at the Royal North Shore Hospital. Now he looked into research and treatment for cancer patients, specialising in breast cancer whenever he could. A close family had been shaken to the core, but emerged stronger and closer than ever as Janelle recovered.

When her mother's condition was sufficiently improved, Nicole went back to work, first appearing in *Archer's Adventure* – based on the true story of the first horse to win the Melbourne Cup. This was followed by another film, *Windrider*, in which Nicole performed her first nude scenes and her first sex scenes. The film was not a success, although it did provide Nicole with her first serious boyfriend, Tom Burlinson, her partner in the on-screen sex scenes.

Nicole would later sum up *Windrider* by saying: "On *Windrider* I met someone who I had a relationship with for three years which was really important to me and helped me to grow. So you've got to look at things positively. I did do some things that weren't of really high-quality, but I learnt a lot."

Burlinson was a successful actor by the time Nicole met him on the set of *Windrider*, his breakthrough role had been in *The Man From Snowy River* in 1981. Dark, handsome and 12 years her senior, Nicole was later to credit Burlinson as the man who gave her a strong belief in men. For a time the pair were Australia's golden couple, both dedicated to their careers and enjoying their time together. Nicole's star was beginning to shine and she was very close to landing the role that would change her career.

Mini-series *Vietnam* showed Australia what Nicole Kidman was capable of. Tackling the issues surrounding Australia's involvement in the Vietnam conflict, 19-year-old Nicole played Megan Goddard – who ages through the series from a 14-year-old schoolgirl to a 24-year-old anti-war protester. The series is not easy on the eye, containing scenes of rape and murder and heavyweight political themes. Nicole later told *Cosmopolitan* magazine: "It really made a big difference to me to work with a three-dimensional character and flesh out the comic and dramatic aspects of the role."

This was also the role for which Nicole began her in-depth character-research, an acting technique that she maintains to this day. Rather than simply learn her lines, Nicole looks into the history of a character, trying to get into their mind. For *Vietnam*, not only did she look into the politics and history of her country's involvement in the conflict, but she also learnt how to perform the dances of the time.

All her hard work paid off handsomely, and Nicole won an Australian Film Institute Award for Best Actress for her work as Megan in *Vietnam*. This was the moment of clarification for Nicole – she knew from that moment that acting was the only life for her.

3

Making her name

NICOLE KIDMAN

MAKING HER NAME

A t the age of 19, Nicole Kidman was already an established film and television actress in Australia. Tall, confident and extremely talented, she was happy in her relationship with Tom Burlinson and her mother was recovering well from the breast cancer that had so shocked the close-knit family.

Nicole's next project *Watch the Shadows Dance*, also known as *Nightrider*, was a martial arts movie that featured a graphic shot of drugs being injected as well as some gratuitous violence. The story mixed paintball gangs and drug-pushers, and included lots of fighting. Nicole's character was

MAKING HER NAME

spunky and independent. It was not a bad movie, but was quickly forgotten as Nicole began filming her next job.

Un'Australiana A Roma features Nicole – as the title suggests – as an Australian in Rome, and was shot for Australian television company ABC in Italy in early 1987. The plotline has Nicole's character Jill caught between two lovers, something which appeared to delight the young actress.

Although she appeared to be having fun filming in Europe, Nicole later admitted that there was a lot more work involved than she had originally let on as well as a communication problem. Director of *Un'Australiana A Roma*, Sergio Martino, spoke no English whatsoever – and neither did the majority of the crew – and so Nicole had to have an interpreter with her on-set at all times.

However, Nicole did have something to distract her while she struggled with the language barrier in Italy. She had been sent a script that inspired her at once. It was essentially a three-handed drama at sea, and it would change both her career and her life.

The film was *Dead Calm* and it already had an unusual history. Originally optioned by Lucille Ball's husband Desi Arnaz, Charles Williams' 1963 novel then fell into the capable hands of Orson

MAKING HER NAME

Welles, who began shooting it with Laurence Harvey and Jeanne Moreau in the cast. Tragedy struck, however, when Harvey died on location and the entire project was shelved.

Terry Hayes – writer of the new version of Williams' story – claims he had Nicole in mind while he worked on the script. This may be the case, however the role of Rae Ingram does not appear, on the surface, to have been written for Nicole. Rae is a 36-year-old married woman who has just lost her five-year-old son in a car accident. This was certainly going to be a challenging part for Nicole, still only 19, to pull off. Also, her husband John was to be played by Sam Neill who, at 20 years her senior, was more than twice Nicole's age.

However, there would certainly be advantages of playing opposite an actor of Sam Neill's reputation. Born in Northern Ireland, Neill's parents moved him back to their native New Zealand when he was seven. Prior to making *Dead Calm* he had appeared in *A Cry in the Dark* with Meryl Streep, *Strong Medicine* with Dick Van Dyke and Douglas Fairbanks Jr, and *The Good Wife*, directed by Ken Cameron, who would later direct Nicole in *Bangkok Hilton*. Neill went on to

MAKING HER NAME

appear in *Jurassic Park* and *The Piano*.

Director Phillip Noyce was originally not eager for Nicole to play the part, mainly because he had never heard of her and had envisioned some famous name such as Meryl Steep or Sigourney Weaver playing the role. However, he changed his mind after watching some tapes of Nicole performing. He later said: "We had our choice of actresses really, even someone with a big box office name. But I looked at tapes of Nicole in *Vietnam* and felt she had the purity we were looking for."

The plot centred around the Ingrams' decision to take an extended yachting trip to try and recover emotionally from the tragic death of their son. While they are at sea they rescue Hughie Warrinder (played by Billy Zane) from a sinking vessel, the other occupants of which, Warrinder tells the couple, have died of food poisoning. At this point the film splits into two stories as John goes aboard the sinking schooner, discovers the awful truth and has to try and escape, while his wife is literally trapped between the devil and the deep blue sea, struggling with a mad man on the yacht.

Nicole saw in her character a surviving spirit. In keeping with her feminist upbringing, the fiery

MAKING HER NAME

redhead refused to play Rae as simply a damsel in distress. Rather than give this stereotypical performance, Nicole wanted to demonstrate Rae's inner strength, and how it is developed throughout the movie.

Once again, Nicole threw herself into the preparation for the role. Not only did she arrive on location early so she could learn to sail the 80-foot-yacht, but she also met with mothers who had lost children, trying to imagine their sense of loss. The hard work paid off, and she even found herself dreaming about having a little boy of her own, even believing it to be true for the first few moments on waking.

But it would take more than emotional preparation to get ready for the *Dead Calm* shoot that was exhausting for its actors physically as well as emotionally. For a start, Nicole suffered from seasickness, although she claims that Sam Neill had it worse, and the redhead's fair skin turned an unflattering shade of pink from the constant exposure to the elements.

During filming Nicole and Billy Zane stayed clear of each other when they were not filming. This was not due to any personal disagreements, but rather a fear of becoming too comfortable with one another to portray such violence and emotion on-screen. By remaining strangers, Nicole and Zane managed to create an air of fear and hatred which is one of the film's strongest elements. Nicole explained this technique by saying that she didn't feel she could be "buddy-buddy" with someone one minute, then convincingly show animosity between them on-screen.

Billy Zane was only really starting out on his career when he appeared in *Dead Calm*, with only small previous roles in *Back to the Future* and *Critters*, plus a handful of TV appearances to his name. His brooding good looks would soon help create a star out of him, and future roles in *Memphis Belle*, *The Phantom* and *Titanic* were to be his.

Although the actors stayed on Hamilton Island, weeks at a time were spent on the water, and the whole shoot took more than three months to complete.

Filming was not without its perks, however, although these seemed to fall to Nicole's co-stars. Both Neill and Zane met their future wives on the *Dead Calm* set. Neill fell for make-up artist Noriko Watanabe, to whom he is still married, while Zane married actress Lisa Collins very swiftly after meeting her, although their union

MAKING HER NAME

was only to last until 1995.

However, all the sweat and tears, all the bruises, seasickness and scrapes would be worth it. *Dead Calm* met with a strong positive reaction when it was released in America in 1989, with many critics picking up on the strength of Nicole's performance. This would be the film that would make the American industry notice Nicole, but she had more films to make before then.

Spotlight on... *Dead Calm*

The role that introduced Nicole to America – and caught the eye of one Tom Cruise – was one that she nearly did not get. Fortunately her powerful performances in projects such as *Vietnam* convinced director Phillip Noyce that Nicole possessed the emotional maturity for the role, despite the fact she was only 19-years-old.

Dead Calm tells the story of John and Rae Ingram (Sam Neill and Nicole) who go sailing to try and recover from an automobile accident that killed their son. Their peace – or 'dead calm' is interrupted when they see a sinking schooner. The lone survivor, Hughie (Billy Zane), boards their boat and tells them what happened.

When John decides to go back over to the schooner to see whether there are any more survivors he gets a nasty shock. Hughie has killed all the other passengers, and now he is alone with Rae, steering the yacht away and leaving John stranded on the sinking ghost ship.

Rae has to fight the killer alone, while John has to escape and try and get back to his wife. With a surprise twist at the end, it is easy to see why this film won Nicole a whole new American fan base. Noyce directs a tight, tense thriller and Nicole puts in a powerful performance as Rae. There is a rape scene involving her character and Hughie which must have been extremely difficult for the young actress to film.

The movie was nominated for seven Australian Film Institute Awards, of which it won four. Director Phillip Noyce went on to direct *Patriot Games* (1992) with Harrison Ford, *The Bone Collector* (1999) with Denzel Washington and Angelina Jolie and *The Quiet American* (2002) with Michael Caine, which won Caine Golden Globe, Bafta and Oscar nominations.

Billy Zane and Sam Neill both met their future wives on the set of *Dead Calm*. Zane then

MAKING HER NAME

went on to appear as Val Kozlowski in *Memphis Belle* (1990) and Caledon Hockley in *Titanic* (1997). He has several projects due for release in 2004/5.

Sam Neill had already appeared in several quality films before *Dead Calm*, but his greater roles came later in films such as *The Hunt for Red October* (1990), *The Piano* (1993), *Jurassic Park* (1993), *The Horse Whisperer* (1998) and *Jurassic Park III* (2001). His role in *The Piano* saw him nominated for an Australian Film Institute Award.

4

Flirting with success

NICOLE KIDMAN

FLIRTING WITH SUCCESS

Before Nicole enjoyed the huge success of Dead Calm, she made two Australian films called *The Bit Part* and *Emerald City*, filmed in 1987 and 1988. Both were comical, cynical tales of the show business world. In *The Bit Part*, Nicole's character Mary McAllister sets the tone of the film when she states: "I don't object to nudity – just exploitative nudity."

Nicole's performance as Helen – "a walking male fantasy" – in *Emerald City* earned her another Australian Film Institute Award nomination. Of the trophy girlfriend role, so unlike her previous roles, Nicole said: "I play a girl who wears beautiful

NICOLE KIDMAN

FLIRTING WITH SUCCESS

clothes and is terribly ambitious." To her credit, Nicole refuses to allow her character to become a bimbo. Her performance also won high praise from film critic Christine Cremen, who wrote of Nicole: "If I was an actress I would be really scared of her. She is going to get all the best roles."

Despite having begun her performing career in amateur theatre, Nicole had not trodden the boards since her film career took off. So she was understandably nervous when she announced that she was going to play Shelby in the Yark Theatre's 1988 production of *Steel Magnolias*, to be directed by Jon Ewing. The production also featured performances from experienced stage actresses Nancye Hayes, Maggie Dence, Pat McDonald, Mellissa Jaffer and Genevieve Lemon.

"My character is a tough introduction to the rigours of live performance," said Nicole in the local press shortly before opening night. "She is on-stage for the duration of the play and is, in effect, a headstrong girl who is accustomed to getting her own way."

Nicole need not have worried. Her performance – in the role that Julia Roberts would later take in the film version – was praised by critics, and she was also nominated for the Sydney Theatre Critics' Best

FLIRTING WITH SUCCESS

Newcomer Award. Although she would not return to the theatre for another ten years, Nicole has proved herself more than capable should she choose to follow a career on the stage rather than before the camera.

As well as her professional successes, there were two major occurrences in Nicole's personal life in 1988. The first, her 21st birthday, was celebrated with a quiet family meal due to her appearances in *Steel Magnolias*. She admitted to the press that she didn't really feel 21. Having worked in the industry for so long, she said that sometimes she felt older, although emotionally sometimes much younger.

Whether Nicole meant that she was not emotionally ready for a relationship is unclear, however she and Tom Burlinson went their separate ways in September 1988, making headlines in the Australian gossip columns. *The Australian Daily Mirror* reported: "After a three-year relationship, actors Tom Burlinson and Nicole Kidman have split... The popular young thespians who, because of work commitments, have seen little of each other for the past six months, told friends of the split a few weeks ago."

Later in the year Nicole would begin dating

FLIRTING WITH SUCCESS

another actor, 25-year-old Marcus Graham. Son of character actor Ron Graham, Marcus had appeared in mini-series *Shadows of the Heart*, as well as theatre roles in productions of *Biloxi Blues*, *Heartbreak Kid* and *The Rivers of China*. His big break came when he was cast in the soap opera *E Street* as Wheels, a bitter young man who is confined to a wheelchair after a motorcycle accident. As his *E Street* role put him firmly in the public eye, for a while Marcus Graham and Nicole were Australia's new golden couple.

Then promotional work for *Dead Calm* took Nicole to America. While she was there she signed with the agent Sam Cohn – who also represented Meryl Streep, Sigourney Weaver and Woody Allen. When Nicole said she got a good response there, she really was understating the point. Her career was heading into orbit now, and Marcus Graham was being left behind.

Kennedy Miller, the company behind *Vietnam*, had another project ready for Nicole, although this time it was a starring role in a vehicle created especially for her. Written by Terry Hayes, the man behind *Dead Calm*, the six hour, $5-million-mini-series *Bangkok Hilton* is a hard-hitting story of a girl – from a stable family environment – tricked into importing drugs to an Asian country and then jailed for it. It was directed by Ken Cameron and filmed in Sydney, Bangkok and Goa. Nicole admitted that the jail scenes were emotionally and physically draining to film. Her hair and make-up for the prison scenes consisted of having dirt put beneath her nails, bags under her eyes and oil brushed through her hair to give it an unwashed appearance. Added to the depressing material she was working with, and the grim jail sets and Nicole was in a thoroughly dark mood while filming these scenes, which she made work for her and her character, channelling her emotions through the scripted lines.

On location in Thailand, Nicole visited a black-market snake farm and let a boa constrictor be placed about her neck. This is not as out of character as it may sound, for Nicole is fond of extreme sports and dangerous activities, a trait she would later share with husband Tom Cruise. Although an early attempt to go skydiving was thwarted by her mother's refusal to sign the permission form, this did not stop Nicole in later years, and as well as leaping from aeroplanes, she has also scaled volcanos and had a couple of near-death experiences.

NICOLE KIDMAN

FLIRTING WITH SUCCESS

Snakes aside, Nicole spent very little time enjoying herself while filming *Bangkok Hilton*, feeling that socialising would bring her out of character. Everyone else who worked on the mini-series had nothing but praise for Nicole and her professionalism, and her performance in the mini-series won her another Australian Film Institute Award.

Around this time Nicole was asked about those actresses who inspired her, and the women she looked up to. Katharine Hepburn was top of the list. Nicole gleefully related a tale when Hepburn pointed out to Spencer Tracy that she was taller than him, and Tracy replied: "Don't worry, I'll cut you down to size." Nicole has always had respect for men who were not afraid to date taller women.

Other heroines of the young performer included Ingrid Bergman, Vanessa Redgrave, Ava Gardner and Jane Fonda – but this would not be merely a list of actors for Nicole has always had a keen political interest, doubtlessly honed by those family discussions around the dining table. She admitted that she admired Margaret Thatcher – although for what she had achieved as a woman rather than her politics – as well as former prime minister of Pakistan Benazir Bhutto for getting where she did. Other influences included Australian film producers

NICOLE KIDMAN

FLIRTING WITH SUCCESS

Pat Lovell and Margaret Fink, who pioneered at a
time when women were finding it hard to break
into the film-making side of the industry.

After *Bangkok Hilton*, Hollywood was calling,
but before she was ready to answer, Nicole had one
more film to do, which would reunite her with
director John Duigan, who had so hated Nicole's
wild red hair when he directed her in an episode of
Winners. This time he solved the problem by
having Nicole wear a long blonde wig to portray
Nicola Radcliffe – "every schoolboy's fantasy, and
the schoolgirl the other girls love to hate" – in the
coming-of-age drama *Flirting*.

Flirting was a sequel to Duigan's 1987 film
The Year My Voice Broke, and featured an unusual
role for Nicole, if only for the fact that she was
playing someone younger than herself. Her co-stars
would be Thandie Newton, Noah Taylor and
Nicole's friend Naomi Watts. Working with Nicole
was eye-opening for Watts, who remembered
noticing how focussed and dedicated she was.

Newton – the daughter of a Zimbabwean
tribal princess – was making her film debut at the
tender age of 15 in the role of Thandiwe, the only
black pupil at an all-girls' school. Nicole plays the
head prefect with secrets, who eventually bonds

FLIRTING WITH SUCCESS

with Thandiwe over the subject of boys. Nicole has a wonderful scene when she describes allowing a workman to touch her. "I'd be trembling so much my legs would have given way," her character tells a shocked Thandiwe. "Afterwards, I'd be reading a lesson convinced all the teachers would know because I was so shivery delicious all over." Nicole's maturity and sensuality comes through the lines and she seems to tap into a well of sexuality that she had not used before, but that would stand her in very good stead in the future.

Flirting was a success worldwide, earning such plaudits as "brilliant" from the *Washington Post*, and "one of the year's best films" from the *Chicago Sun-Times*. However, the year in question was rather later, as *Flirting* was not released in America until 1991, by which time Nicole was already a well-known resident there.

Because, while Nicole was filming *Flirting*, over in Hollywood Tom Cruise was sitting down to watch *Dead Calm* at a private screening. He had heard rumours about this Nicole Kidman and wanted to see what all the fuss was about. Legend has it that at the end of the movie Cruise leaned over to his friend and whispered: "Who's that girl? I have to make a film with her."

5

Tom & Nicole

TOM & NICOLE

When Nicole first heard that Tom Cruise wanted to see her in America regarding a possible part in his next film, *Days of Thunder*, her first reaction was: "I thought, 'Oh yeah, right'. I'd been to America before. You go in, you audition, you don't get the job." What Nicole did not realise at that time was that the job didn't exist, the character in the film would be created especially for her.

It is easy to understand why this sudden turn of events was a little hard for Nicole to believe. Although she had enjoyed success in Australia, and *Dead Calm* had taken her talents to a wider

TOM & NICOLE

audience, this was an personal invitation from an A-List Hollywood movie star. Tom Cruise's star was shining brightly in 1989 after appearing in some of the Eighties' highest-grossing and most popular movies. At 28-years-old, the former Thomas Cruise Mapother IV was already as famous as they come.

His rise to fame had not come easily. Cruise had a difficult childhood, never being allowed to settle in one place for too long on account of his father's engineering job that meant Cruise, his mother Mary Lee, and his three sisters were constantly on the move. The family lived in seven different places before Cruise was 12-years-old. The child also suffered from dyslexia, and was treated badly before the condition was recognised. Cruise remembered that he felt ashamed when he was put in remedial reading classes and that the other children at school made fun of him. He conceded though, that the experience made him tougher emotionally.

The moving stopped when Mary Lee divorced Cruise's father when Cruise was just 12. When he was interviewed Cruise recalled being hit hard by his parents separation. "After a divorce you feel so vulnerable," he said. "And travelling the way I did,

TOM & NICOLE

you're closed off a lot from other people... I went through a period after the divorce of really wanting to be accepted, wanting love and attention from people. But I never really seemed to fit in anywhere."

A religious youngster, Cruise enrolled in the St Francis Seminary at the age of 14 to train as a priest, but dropped out after just a year. The brothers there began to suspect that his interest in the priesthood was waning when they caught Cruise sneaking out of the dormitory to meet girls. Cruise would later become devoted to the Church of Scientology, when he married Mimi Rogers.

The young boy's next passion was wrestling, and it was not until a knee injury prevented him from competing in a high school wrestling team event that Tom Cruise discovered acting. At Glen Ridge High School, New Jersey, Cruise landed the role of Nathan Detroit in the musical *Guys and Dolls* – and he discovered where his true talent lay. A comment from a talent scout after a performance convinced Cruise to go for performing as a career.

He made his film debut at the age of 18 in a seven-minute-appearance in *Endless Love*, which starred Brooke Shields and Martin Hewitt. After this speedy start, Cruise swiftly rose through the Hollywood ranks with well-polished performances in *Risky Business* and *All the Right Moves*. Women began to fall for the 5'7" actor with the cheeky grin – now perfected by dental surgery – while men also enjoyed his films, giving Cruise the reputation of being both a man's man and a ladies' man – all in all a difficult combination to resist.

In 1986 came the role that was going to catapult Cruise into the big time, as Lt Pete 'Maverick' Mitchell in *Top Gun*. Also featuring Kelly McGillis, Val Kilmer and Anthony Edwards, *Top Gun* tells the story of an elite training school for fighter pilots. The film was a massive success and the soundtrack, featuring Berlin's *Take My Breath Away*, sold in its millions. Cruise followed this hit with roles in high-grossing movies such as *The Colour of Money, Rain Man, Cocktail* and *Born on the Fourth of July* – for which he received his first Oscar nomination, for Best Actor in a Leading Role.

So it was a very successful and confident Cruise that Nicole Kidman met in Hollywood. Nicole has spoken about her instant attraction to her future husband, but what worried her most on their first meeting was the difference between their heights, fearing that they might choose another actress who wouldn't tower over him for the role.

However, following the meeting Nicole was offered the part. When she asked about the height difference the producers told her that if it didn't bother Cruise, it wasn't a problem for them either. By showing such disregard for her height, and such confidence in himself, Tom Cruise was already making quite an impression on Nicole.

And so Nicole had won herself a part in her first Hollywood film, alongside one of the biggest stars of the previous decade. And although the role was a 'girlfriend role', this girlfriend was at least a neurosurgeon.

Days of Thunder is a Tom Cruise vehicle about a NASCAR driver who has to face some serious facts when he and his main rival crash on the track and are taken to hospital. Cruise's character learns that his rival is seriously injured and finishes the film taking his place on the track. In a film that is marked by the somewhat ridiculous character names, Cruise plays Cole Trickle, his rival is Rowdy Burns and his mentor is Harry Hogge, played by Robert Duvall. Nicole's character gets off rather lightly with the moniker Dr Claire Lewicki.

TOM & NICOLE

Using her own accent and sporting a head of wildly corkscrewing red hair, Nicole shines in her scenes with Cruise, sharing the banter during the comic romantic moments, and with her eyes flashing fire during her "infantile egomaniac" speech, when she remonstrates with him for thinking he can control what happens on the track.

Despite popular belief, Nicole and Cruise did not begin their romance straight away. Nicole was still involved with Marcus Graham, at home in Australia, although this relationship did not last much longer, and Cruise was in the middle of a separation from his wife Mimi Rogers. Cruise and Rogers had been married in 1987, by which time she had already appeared in the film *Blue Skies Again* and the television series *Paper Dolls*. Roles would follow for her in *Gung Ho*, *Someone to Watch Over Me* and *Streetsmart*.

Soon the paparazzi were buzzing around the co-stars, searching for the gossip. Pictures of Nicole on Cruise's Harley Davidson were splashed across the papers and magazines. For her part, Nicole dismissed rumours firmly and politely, saying that she was supporting her friend Cruise through a difficult time in his personal life.

Cruise later said that he and Nicole did not

begin their romance until his relationship with Mimi Rogers was completely over. He said it would not have been ethical to start a new relationship until his divorce.

He filed for divorce in 1990 and a joint statement was released to the press stating: "While there have been positive aspects to our marriage, there were some issues which could not be resolved, even after working on them for a period of time." Although Nicole and Cruise continued to deny their romance for a little while longer, more and more paparazzi shots of Tom's car outside Nicole's apartment were making their way into the press. Nicole also announced that she was moving to America permanently.

Nicole's mother Janelle met Cruise for the first time when she visited her daughter in February 1990. He was obviously keen to make a good impression, flying her in on a private Lear jet. Janelle had been surprised to discover the identity of Nicole's boyfriend, and had prepared herself for meeting him by watching him in *Born on the Fourth of July*, where she had been moved to tears by his passionate performance.

On 26 March the golden couple attended the Oscars together, along with Cruise's mother Mary

TOM & NICOLE

Lee. This was regarded as their 'coming out' event to the press regarding their relationship. The following month, with filming finished on *Days of Thunder*, they took a holiday in the Bahamas. Watching Cruise racing cars for the film had made Nicole realise they shared a passion for extreme activities, which was compounded by his taking her for a spin around the track at 180 miles per hour. In the Bahamas they swam with stingrays and moray eels. Later, to celebrate the opening of *Days of Thunder*, they took Mary Lee skydiving.

Nicole would later say that she and Cruise shared their first, brief kiss – their first as themselves rather than performing before the cameras that is – during a parachute jump. Having found a man who like his thrills as much as she did, Nicole would also say that Cruise was impressed by her own willingness to jump out of an aeroplane with him.

But the thrilling experiences were only just beginning. Next was a trip back to Australia so Cruise could meet Antony and the rest of Nicole's family. By all accounts the trip went well, although the increase in press attention in her homeland scared and shocked Nicole. But it was something she knew she had to get used to, as she had accepted a

TOM & NICOLE

proposal of marriage from Tom Cruise.

After a romance lasting less than a year, Tom Cruise and Nicole Kidman were married on Christmas Eve 1990, in a house they had rented in Telluride, Colorado. Nicole wore the dress she had bought years before in Amsterdam. Nicole's sister Antonia was her bridesmaid, and the guests were mainly family, although Cruise's co-star from *Rain Man*, Dustin Hoffman was there.

Later, Nicole denied rumours that she had to convert to Scientology to marry Cruise. She was adamant that she wouldn't have married him if he had tried to force his beliefs on her. She did add that although she didn't follow just one philosophy, she found parts of Scientology very interesting.

Indeed, Nicole also admitted around this time that her marriage had given her a new confidence that she had previously lacked. She developed more faith in herself and her performances and started to enjoy her success more.

Although she did not get the role she auditioned for in *Ghost*, she was about to prove her ability with her next project, *Billy Bathgate,* that would pair her with Dustin Hoffman. She was, in fact, called upon to prove herself almost immediately to director Robert Benton, whose

TOM & NICOLE

previous work included *Kramer vs Kramer*. Nicole was cast on the condition that she could master a convincing American accent, and Benton was sceptical about her pulling it off.

Benton, however, had to concede that Nicole's American accent was perfect. The biggest problem was that the crew thought she was larking around when she reverted to her natural Australian accent at the end of a day's shooting.

With her thoroughly convincing accent, Nicole plays a gangster's moll with a difference. Her character Drew Preston is a socialite who is drawn to the seedy thrill of dating those involved in organised crime. The part called for nudity, but Nicole did not flinch from it. She may have been playing another 'girlfriend role' but she gave it her all. She would later comment that working with Dustin Hoffman was better than three years of drama training.

Once filming for *Billy Bathgate* was finished, Nicole could finally spend some time with her husband and make up for the honeymoon they missed because of her filming commitments. "We both have gypsy blood in our veins," she said. "I want to do some serious travelling in Africa and spend a lot more time scuba-diving and horse-riding." As far as the horse-riding was concerned, Nicole was to get plenty of that in her next picture.

Director Ron Howard had originally approached Cruise about *Far and Away*, then called *Irish Story*, back in 1983. When the time was right for both actor and director it seemed perfect casting to have Cruise's new wife in the lead female role. The plot concerned Shannon Christie and Joseph Donnelly, Irish immigrants of 1892. The film follows them from Ireland to America as they work to make their dreams come true, falling in love along the way. The finished film is stunning to look at, with rolling landscapes and period costumes.

Director Ron Howard was certainly a familiar face, having played Ritchie Cunningham in *Happy Days* for several years. Since the late Seventies, however, he had been stretching himself as a director, with *Splash*, *Cocoon*, *Willow* and *Backdraft* to his credit. After *Far and Away* he would continue making a name for himself with *Apollo 13* and *Ransom*, before winning the Oscars for Best Director and Best Picture with *A Beautiful Mind*.

Howard won the trust of both Nicole and

Cruise by treating them as individuals, and encouraging them to come to him rather than each other with questions regarding the film. "He said to us at the beginning, 'I don't want you both going through each other and directing each other. I want you to always come to me,'" Nicole said, when recalling the making of the film. "That set up a very good working relationship because we had to include the director and not go off and play married couples."

However, Howard was not above using little tricks to get the shot he wanted. The most famous example of this is when Cruise's Joseph is lying naked and unconscious, with just a pudding bowl to cover his modesty, and Nicole's Shannon takes a peek under the bowl. But Howard was not getting the reaction he wanted from Nicole. Cruise had been using a piece of black cloth to cover his groin area, and Howard felt that there was something to be done about that.

At Howard's prompting, Cruise removed the cloth before one take and Nicole's genuinely surprised and awed reaction was the hilarious cut that was used in the final film.

Another incident on the set involved the horses that Nicole was so looking forward to riding, however riding them in full period costume – complete with corset and bloomers – proved not so easy. There was also fierce competition between Nicole and her husband as to who would ride the quickest, with each of them checking with the wranglers who was the fastest.

Shot in Ireland, the production provided Nicole and Cruise with a working honeymoon. They embraced the laid-back Irish way of life, even becoming regulars in the local Paidi O'Se pub.

Howard would later say of his leading lady: "It pissed me off when people were dismissive of Nicole because she was married to Tom. She handled it so beautifully. I was so frustrated for her. But talent will out..."

Although Nicole still had a way to go before she was completely out of her husband's shadow, she was most certainly on her way. The next few years would provide her with starring vehicles of her own, as well as some family developments. However, for some time between *Far and Away* and her next project, *Malice*, Nicole found herself out of work – an unusual and uncomfortable situation for an actress. The worrying time cannot have been made easier by the fact that Cruise was filming *A Few Good Men*, a huge movie where he got top billing, despite starring opposite such famous names as Jack Nicholson, Demi Moore, Kevin Bacon and Kiefer Sutherland.

"I went through a period when I didn't get any work for a year," Nicole said in an interview. "It was a very tough time for me and I wanted to go back to Australia, but Tom's career was in America. I was willing to give up a lot of other things to keep my marriage." Fortunately the work-drought did not last too long.

TOM & NICOLE

Spotlight on... Tom Cruise

Nicole's husband of a decade was by far the more famous of the two when they married in 1990. And while Nicole's star rose and rose, Cruise has maintained his position in the Hollywood A-List. He was ranked number three in *Empire* magazine's Top 100 Movie Stars of All Time in 1997, reached number 14 in *Premiere* magazine's annual Power 100 List in 2003 and in the same year placed at number four in *Star TV*'s Top 10 Box Office Stars of the 1990s. He has been nominated for three Oscars and six Golden Globes.

In more recent years, Cruise has broadened his horizons by producing films as well as starring in them – his producer/executive producer credits include *Mission: Impossible* (1996) and its 2000 sequel, *Vanilla Sky* (2001), *The Last Samurai* (2003) as well as Nicole's *The Others* in 2001.

From the start women across the world were won over by his all-American good looks and easy smile. Cruise then stopped himself from being just another pretty boy actor, and assured himself a place in film history, when he also impressed the male members of the

TOM & NICOLE

audience with his macho characters in classic Eighties' films such as *Risky Business*, *All the Right Moves*, and the infamous *Top Gun*.

He has appeared alongside such stars as Paul Newman in 1986's *The Colour of Money*. Newman was the one to introduce Cruise to a state of more political awareness, which led the younger actor to take the role in director Oliver Stone's anti-war film *Born on the Fourth of July*, for which he would win a Golden Globe, as well as receiving Oscar and Bafta nominations. Being politically motivated is something that Cruise and Nicole would have in common. During their marriage they donated to Hillary Clinton's senate campaign.

Other notable co-stars have been Brad Pitt (*Interview With a Vampire*), Dustin Hoffman (*Rain Man*), Gene Hackman (*The Firm*) and Jack Nicholson, Demi Moore, Kevin Bacon and Kiefer Sutherland (*A Few Good Men*). The latter won him a Golden Globe nomination.

Cruise has successfully fought against stereotyping in his career, especially with his performance as Lestat de Lioncourt in 1994's *Interview With the Vampire: The Vampire Chronicles*. Anne Rice, the author of the book on

which the film was based, did not think Cruise
was the right actor to play the depraved bisexual
vampire Lestat, preferring the actor Rutger
Haüer. However, after seeing the film Rice wrote
Cruise a letter to apologise and publicly took
back her objections, so won over was she with
Cruise's portrayal.

Indeed, Cruise is electrifying as the
vampire devoid of morals. With long blonde
hair it was a physical transformation as well as
a change of character – from the all-American
hero type to the killer vampire who transforms
a young girl – played by Kirsten Dunst – into a
sadistic vampire.

After *Interview With the Vampire*, Cruise
went to work making the first of the *Mission:
Impossible* movies. Inspired by the television
series that began in 1966, this film saw Cruise
playing secret agent Ethan Hunt. He would
later follow this blockbuster – directed by Brian
De Palma – with a sequel in 2000. *Mission:
Impossible 3* is currently in production and is
slated for a 2005 release date.

After that came *Jerry Maguire*, which saw
Cruise playing a sports agent who is fired after
an attack of conscience sees him criticising the

TOM & NICOLE

firm he works for. Left with just one client, American footballer Rod Tidwell – Cuba Gooding Jr on Oscar-winning form – and former secretary Dorothy Boyd (Renee Zellweger), Jerry Maguire has to rebuild his career and his life.

The 1996 feelgood film was a huge hit. Cruise was nominated for another Oscar, and won a Golden Satellite Award, a Golden Globe and an MTV Movie Award. Next was *Eyes Wide Shut* with Nicole, and then *Magnolia* with Julianna Moore, which also won Cruise a Golden Globe and an Oscar nomination.

A look at the way nine different lives interact in one day, *Magnolia* sees Cruise playing Frank TJ Mackey, the son of Jason Robards' character, who hates women and teaches a seminar on how to love and dump them. This film marked a move away from blockbuster territory for Cruise, and won him critical acclaim.

Vanilla Sky was released in 2001, after Cruise and Nicole had separated. Cruise and his leading lady Penelope Cruz would enter into a relationship that was to last until 2004. Also appearing in the film alongside Cruise and Cruz was Cameron Diaz, Kurt Russell and Jason Lee.

Vanilla Sky was directed by Cameron

TOM & NICOLE

Crowe and was a remake of the 1997 film *Abre Los Ojos*, in which Penelope Cruz had also starred. *Abre Los Ojos* was directed by Alejandro Amenabar, who was also the director of Nicole's *The Others*, on which Cruise was a producer. This complicated state of affairs meant that Cruise did attend the premiere of *The Others*, but he and Nicole kept their distance from each other rather than fuel the gossip columns further.

2002 saw Cruise starring in the Steven Spielberg directed blockbuster hit *Minority Report*. Based on a short story by Philip K Dick, the film is set in the future when murderers are arrested before they have committed their crimes using technology which sees the future. However, when Cruise's cop character Detective John Anderton gets the tables turned when he is accused of a future crime. Colin Farrell was a co-star.

Another blockbuster was to follow in 2003 with *The Last Samurai*, directed by Edward Zwick, which Cruise also produced. Cruise plays Captain Nathan Algren a military advisor who is captured in battle and adopts the culture of the Samurai who he was previously fighting against. Cruise spent two years preparing for this role, for which he learnt how to use a Samurai sword and speak Japanese.

Collateral, Cruise's next project, concerns a taxi driver who is taken hostage by a contract killer and is due for a 2004 release. Other future plans include *Mission: Impossible 3, The Few* and *War of the Worlds*. If Cruise's track record is anything to go by, they will all be huge hits.

6

Power couple

NICOLE KIDMAN

POWER COUPLE

However happy Nicole was in her marriage, she was still a working actress. Directed by Harold Becker, the film *Malice* appeared at just the right time for Nicole, ending a dry period where she had auditioned plenty, but not worked. This film featured a strong cast, which included Bill Pullman, Alec Baldwin, Anne Bancroft, Bebe Neuwirth and a young Gwyneth Paltrow in a minor role.

Nicole was to play Tracy Kennsinger, partner of Bill Pullman's character Andy Safian, and a woman who changes dramatically throughout the course of the movie. With a plot that covered serial killers on campus, botched operations, double lives and one too many far-fetched twists, the film was not a success, although Nicole worked well in her dramatic scenes when her character gets angry and wants revenge. This was a darker side to Nicole, that she had not had the chance to demonstrate in America before, and it would stand her in good stead for future performances.

However, before any more films were to be considered, Cruise and Nicole had a very important matter to attend to. On 22 December, 1992 – two days before their second wedding anniversary – a baby girl was born in Florida. The following month the famous couple adopted that little girl and named her Isabella Jane Kidman Cruise, Bella for short.

"The spiritual aspect of adoption," said Nicole in an interview, "is that it's so extraordinary that two adults and a baby find each other in such a huge world. That makes it very special."

Although both Nicole and Cruise were eager to spend time with Isabella, there was still work to be done. Cruise was filming *The Firm* with Gene Hackman and Jeanne Tripplehorn around this time, and Nicole was getting ready to start work on the tear-jerking drama *My Life*, directed by Bruce Joel Rubin.

NICOLE KIDMAN

POWER COUPLE

The story of *My Life* concerns Michael Keaton's character Bob Jones, who discovers he is suffering from inoperable cancer and has only a short time to live. Nicole plays his wife Gail, who is pregnant with their first child. Although she did not have to reach far into her past to remember her own brush with cancer in the family, Nicole decided that she needed to research the pregnancy part of her role. However, she did not just read up on the pregnancy and birth, she attended a natural birth to see a mother's reactions for herself. This work paid off and Nicole's performance is strong and moving, although Keaton always remains the main focus of a beautiful film about a difficult subject.

Films such as *Malice* and *My Life* were keeping Nicole's face in the spotlight, although it seemed she was always playing the girlfriend or wife of the lead character, rather than the lead role as she had been in Australia, and this inequality was also present in any comparison between her and Cruise where work was concerned. To further stress the difference between her husband's career and her own, Nicole was firmly in the background when Cruise was awarded a star on Hollywood's Walk of Fame in 1993. He then began filming his

POWER COUPLE

role as Lestat de Lioncourt in the movie version of Anne Rice's *Interview With the Vampire: The Vampire Chronicles*, a film that was to take him to a new level of fame.

However, Nicole was also about to make a breakthrough of sorts. Another girlfriend role loomed, but this was definitely one with a difference as her boyfriend was to be a superhero. Nicole's role as Dr Chase Meridian in *Batman Forever* is that of an extremely sexy criminal psychiatrist who attempts to seduce both Batman and millionaire Bruce Wayne, unaware that they are the same man.

Val Kilmer was to play the caped crusader in a film that owed much of its success to the performances of the supporting cast which included, as well as Nicole, Jim Carrey as The Riddler/Edward Nygma, Tommy Lee Jones as Two-Face/Harvey Dent and Chris O'Donnell as Robin/Dick Grayson.

This *Batman* film was also made with a different director to the previous two when Joel Schumacher replaced Tim Burton. Schumacher's Gotham City was not as dark as Burton's, with more room for wisecracks, such as when Batman remarks to Dr Chase Meridian: "It's the car, right? Chicks love the car," and "The Bat Signal is not a beeper."

Nicole Kidman's career has gone from strength to strength. Her roles have taken her from learning to swing on a trapeze for 'Moulin Rouge!' to wearing heavy shackles in 'Dogville', in which she is pictured above.

Nicole Kidman at the London premiere for the 2003 film
'Cold Mountain'. The award-winning film co-starred Jude Law
and Renée Zellwegger.

Nicole Kidman pictured with Tom Cruise.
Cruise saw Kidman in the film 'Dead Calm' and wanted her for
his next project, 'Days of Thunder'. They soon became an item
and married in 1990. They adopted two children, Isabella Jane
and Conor Antony. The couple divorced in 2001.

An unrecognisable Nicole Kidman in her Oscar-winning role as British author Virgina Woolf in 'The Hours' (2002). She does not shy away from playing dislikeable characters and doesn't depend on her glamour to carry a film, as the make-up in this film proves.

NICOLE KIDMAN

POWER COUPLE

Indeed, it was Schumacher who cast Nicole, after initial rumours had linked Sandra Bullock with the role. When asked about his decision at the time, Schumacher smiled and said: "I know she doesn't look anything like a criminal psychiatrist, but it's my Gotham City and I can do what I want. I've had my eye on Nicole since *Dead Calm.*"

Nicole's performance fitted perfectly with the over-the-top feel of the film, helped along by the fantastic mugging of Tommy Lee Jones and Jim Carrey. Although she might have been playing another babe with a brain, at least this time Nicole was showing her sexy side with her slinky black dresses and bright red lipstick, as well as her flair for comedy in a runaway blockbuster.

Nicole's sensuality and comic timing, which had not really been seen in any of her American films before *Batman Forever*, were also to get an airing in her next film, which was also the vehicle providing her with the starring role she needed to prove herself to the American industry and audiences alike. The film that allowed her talents to be seen away from the shadow of her ultra-famous husband, was Gus Van Sant's brilliant *To Die For*.

Van Sant was already well known and respected in the movie-making community for his work on films such as 1989's *Drugstore Cowboy* with Matt Dillon and *My Own Private Idaho* in 1991 with River Phoenix and Keanu Reeves. He would later work with Matt Damon, Ben Affleck and Robin Williams in 1997's award-winning *Good Will Hunting*. Van Sant has always enjoyed a reputation for working outside the system, which was to work in Nicole's favour when it came to casting.

Surprisingly, the role of weathergirl Suzanne Stone Maretto was originally going to be played by Meg Ryan. When she dropped out, Nicole heard about the part and tried to get herself considered, but ran up against preconceived ideas wherever she turned – she was not well enough known, she was not American, she was not the right 'type' for the role. Finally she decided to go straight to the top and telephoned Van Sant himself. "We talked for an hour." Nicole later recalled, "and I told him that it would be a chance that no one had given me in America... He called me back two hours later and gave me the role."

And what a role it was – Nicole was later to describe Suzanne Stone Maretto as "a Barbie doll gone wrong" and she certainly looked the part, with perfect blonde bob, two-piece skirt suits and high heels. The plot of this black comedy concerns

POWER COUPLE

a woman who believes most sincerely that you are only worth something if you are on television. Her ridiculous levels of ambition are matched only by her love of clichés, her earnest belief in what she is saying, and her complete lack of morals. Although Suzanne Stone Maretto is an intensely dislikeable character – who, during the course of the movie, seduces three teenagers into killing her husband – Nicole was brave enough to take on the role, and powerful enough as an actress to bring another level to it.

Supported by a strong cast, Nicole gave a performance that was spot on in its strange mixture of the sinister and the comic. She researched her role by spending three days in a motel, watching talk shows such as Oprah and Rikki Lake.

Unlike her experience on *Billy Bathgate*, this time Nicole used her American accent non-stop from the beginning of rehearsals to the end of filming, never reverting back to her real accent at the end of the day. Such was her involvement with her character that Nicole asked her husband not to visit her on the set. She later explained this decision, saying: "When you're creating a complex character like that, you don't want the person who knows you inside out standing there watching you... Also, he's a very forceful presence on a set, and it's distracting to people."

Filmed in Canada to save money, Nicole's supporting cast included Matt Dillon as her husband Larry, Joaquin Phoenix as her teenage lover, while Casey Affleck and Alison Folland played the two students Suzanne uses in her murderous plot. True to Van Sant's reputation for taking risks, Folland had never acted in anything before, and had only attended the open audition for *To Die For* as a joke. When she got the role the casting directors had trouble finding her because she had not bothered waiting to find out and had flown to the Bahamas on holiday with her parents. However, all Van Sant's gambles paid off and all performances worked well. *To Die For* was the success story of the Cannes Film Festival 1995.

Critics loved Nicole's portrayal of the ice-queen weathergirl and she was rewarded with a whole raft of best actress prizes, including a Golden Globe, the National Film Critics Association Award, a London Critics Circle Award, and an Empire Award. She was also nominated for a BAFTA, an American Comedy Award and the MTV Movie Award for Most Desirable Female – an honour for which she was nominated twice in the same year,

POWER COUPLE

for her roles in *To Die For* and *Batman Forever*.

Although it would be difficult to follow *To Die For* professionally, Nicole's personal life was making headlines all over again in February 1995 when she and Cruise adopted Conor Antony. By adopting a mixed-race baby, the couple spoke out about equality and treating your children as individuals. Nicole also spoke out about her continuing to work, despite now caring for two children under five-years-old, pointing out that her own mother had worked throughout her childhood, and how this had provided Nicole with a strong role model that she could look up to. She also admitted that trying to juggle motherhood and a career was not easy – and it was not about to get any easier as Nicole's next film role was going to be one that would test all her skills.

7

Portrait of a lady

NICOLE KIDMAN

PORTRAIT OF A LADY

B ack in Sydney's amateur theatre scene, then student director Jane Campion had cryptically warned Nicole to protect her talent. Now Campion was a big name after directing 1993's *The Piano* – for which she also won an Oscar for the screenplay – and had been planning to make Henry James' *The Portrait of a Lady* into a film for some time. Nicole had been passionate about being cast as Isabel, but met with early disappointment when Campion looked at the actress's early work in the USA and decided that Nicole was not right for the part.

"Jane saw some of my work that I did in

PORTRAIT OF A LADY

America and said I didn't have the spirit," Nicole later said. "It was almost as if she was saying that I had failed to protect my talent."

Nicole proved that she did have the necessary spirit, however she would have to endure a lengthy audition process first – which was extremely unusual for an actress who was so well-known. Disappointed at having to prove herself, Nicole nevertheless put her heart and soul into trying to get the part. When she finally won the role, the film was suspended twice, first due to the tragic death of Campion's baby son and secondly because of the director's second pregnancy, which resulted in a healthy baby daughter. By the time *The Portrait of a Lady* was ready for filming, Nicole had completed *To Die For* which restored her faith in her own acting abilities that had been tested by some of her early American roles and Campion's original reaction to them.

A stellar cast was assembled for the film. John Malkovich, Richard E Grant, Sir John Gielgud, Viggo Mortensen and Shelley Winters all took part, and Nicole was once again the lead role in a strongly supported movie. As her husband made *Jerry Maguire* and enjoyed the success of *Mission: Impossible*, Nicole was strapping herself into a corset to give herself the 19-inch waist the period piece required.

The Portrait of a Lady is intentionally a difficult film to watch. It concerns Nicole's character Isabel, a wealthy young woman who turns down several proposals of marriage before falling in love with and marrying Osmond (Malkovich), who emotionally abuses and mistreats her.

Campion was rewarded for taking a chance on Nicole. The director later admitted that she had always thought that *she* was the best person to play the part, but that Nicole surprised her by doing stuff that she wouldn't even have thought of.

Although the final film was not a high-grossing one, there was significant critical praise for Nicole's performance, including some calls for an Oscar nomination that were sadly not heeded.

After such hard work on *The Portrait of a Lady*, Nicole needed a break. She made an appearance in her friend John Duigan's *The Leading Man*, it was a very brief cameo as an Academy Award presenter, leaving her free to enjoy some time with her husband and children. A trip to Australia was also on the cards as Nicole's

PORTRAIT OF A LADY

younger sister Antonia was getting married to her entrepreneur boyfriend Angus Hawley in February 1996.

Nicole was her sister's bridesmaid, wearing light blue, while little Isabella was a flower girl. The ceremony was held at the chapel in Monte St Angelo School, North Sydney, where Antonia had been a pupil. A lavish reception followed at Sydney's Museum of Contemporary Arts, although Nicole and Cruise had to leave early to get back to check on baby Conor.

Although Antonia is dark-haired and with an olive-complexion, she and Nicole have extraordinarily similar features, and both have the same tall, willowy build. At the time of her wedding, Antonia was a researcher for a television show, although since then she has become an Australian television personality, presenting several programmes, including one on films for which she interviewed Tom Cruise in 1999. She and Angus Hawley are still married and have three children together.

Rested, relaxed and reconnected with her family, Nicole was ready to go back to work. Her next project was the kind of action-adventure film that the public would more readily associate with Cruise. The first film by DreamWorks SKG – the

PORTRAIT OF A LADY

studio set up by Steven Spielberg, Jeffrey Katzenberg and David Geffen – *The Peacemaker* was to star George Clooney, fresh from his small-screen success as Dr Doug Ross in *ER*. Directed by Mimi Leder, the film was shot in Slovakia, Macedonia and New York, and concerns terrorism, nuclear warheads and saving the world.

Nicole plays Dr Julia Kelly, a nuclear physicist, acting head of the White House Nuclear Smuggling Group and the voice of reason to Clooney's headstrong Lieutenant Colonel Thomas Devoe. The handsome actor was also to become a close friend outside of work. Nicole was the one who called Clooney's commitment-phobic bluff, betting him $10,000 that he would be a father by his 40th birthday. When that occasion came and went with no child in sight, Nicole posted Clooney a cheque, which he returned with a note that read: "Double or nothing – check back with me when I'm 50!"

The Peacemaker was a hit, grossing highly and exploding from the screen in wave after wave of spectacular special effects. Although Clooney steals almost every scene he appears in, Nicole was commended for her role, which steps up a notch for the surprise ending.

By the time she reached her 30th birthday,

NICOLE KIDMAN

PORTRAIT OF A LADY

Nicole had played a neurosurgeon, a nuclear physicist and a criminal psychiatrist, as well as an expectant mother, an abused wife and a murderous weathergirl. She had won many awards and enjoyed much critical success. After a shaky start in a new country, her acting career was certainly on the up, but her personal life was heading for a trying time, followed by a disastrous patch that would leave her badly shaken but ultimately stronger.

8

Rising to the top

RISING TO THE TOP

W hether or not Nicole's next film project with her husband – *Eyes Wide Shut*, directed by Stanley Kubrick – was the beginning of the end of their marriage, there can be no doubt it placed the couple under a great degree of pressure. Shooting began in November 1996 and did not finish until January 1998, after which there were still parts with which the perfectionist Kubrick wanted to reshoot. The film would not reach the big screen until July 1999.

Eyes Wide Shut was adapted by Kubrick and writer Frederic Raphael from Arthur Schnitzler's 1926 book *Traumnovelle*. Updated and moved forward in time, Kubrick felt that only a real-life married couple would be able to convey the intimacy that he was looking for in this tale of sexual discovery. He wrote to both Cruise and Nicole separately to ask them if they would be interested.

It was not surprising that they both replied in the affirmative. Kubrick's long and distinguished directorial career was littered with award-winning, classic films, such as *Spartacus* (1960), *Lolita* (1962), *Dr Strangelove* (1964), *2001: A Space Odyssey* (1968), *A Clockwork Orange* (1971), *The Shining* (1980) and *Full Metal Jacket* (1987). No stranger to controversy, Kubrick also had a reputation for working his actors hard – Jack Nicholson, who worked with him on *The Shining*, famously said: "He gives new meaning to the word meticulous." Nicole was later to confirm this reputation, saying at a press conference: "It's true, he is a perfectionist and that's scary. He expects you to dedicate yourself to the film 200 per cent and nothing less will do."

However, the Cruises were more than ready to work hard in exchange for being part of one of Kubrick's films. The topics involved also represented a change of direction for the couple, and for Cruise in particular, as the film was darker and more art house that his usual action-adventure fare. The plot concerned Cruise's character Dr William Harford and how he reacts upon discovering his wife's sexual fantasies involve other people. This triggers a chain of potentially erotic events, culminating in Harford's presence as a spectator at an orgy.

The film's long over-running shooting schedule took its toll on the cast. Harvey Keitel was the first to leave the production because of scheduling problems. He was replaced in the role of Victor Ziegler by Sydney Pollack. Next to go was Jennifer Jason Leigh, whose commitment to David Cronenberg's film *eXistenZ* meant she was unable to attend reshoots. Her replacement Marie Richardson had to refilm the entire part of Marion Nathanson all over again.

During the lengthy shoot, rumours began to circulate that the Cruise marriage was in trouble. The stories cited the difficult working conditions the couple were experiencing, plus the emotional and sexual content of the material they were working with. Cruise spoke out against the press reports. "Filming *Eyes Wide Shut* could have destroyed our marriage," he admitted, "but instead it brought us together." However, he also

RISING TO THE TOP

spoke about the pressures of such an intense project to journalist Jeff Craig, saying: "I don't like to bring work home, but sometimes, because of the characters and the nature of the scenes, it was very difficult not to think about it and become slightly obsessed with it."

One of the most difficult scenes for Cruise to leave at the studio involved Nicole's character's fantasy about having sex with a naval officer. Cruise did not appear on the set the day the scene was filmed, and it easy to see why. Although the scene is brief, it is probably the most graphically sexual in the film. Nicole later said during the publicity tour for the film: "Stanley wanted it to be harsh and gritty looking, almost pornographic. He didn't exploit me, I did it because I thought it was important to the film. The film deals with sex and sexual obsession and the scenes could not have been of me in a bra and panties... I certainly wouldn't have done it for any other director and, yes, it was a little difficult to go home to my husband afterwards."

The couple had moved to England for the filming and had become very comfortable there, with Conor and Isabella attending the local school near their house in St Albans, Hertfordshire. Much to the delight of the other parents, Nicole and Cruise would frequently pick their children up after classes themselves.

Cruise's role in *Eyes Wide Shut* was three times the length of Nicole's, so it is unsurprising that he was still involved in retakes in the UK while Nicole flew to America to begin shooting her next movie, *Practical Magic*.

Co-starring Sandra Bullock, *Practical Magic* is a light-hearted film about two sisters who are witches and live under a curse that any man they fall in love with is doomed to an untimely death. Directed by Griffin Dunne, the film also featured performances from Stockard Channing, Dianne Wiest, Goran Visnjic and Aidan Quinn. The light-hearted content must have been a relief for Nicole after putting herself through the emotional wringer with *Eyes Wide Shut*, *The Portrait of a Lady* and *To Die For*.

It was Bullock who wanted Nicole for the role of the wilder sister, Gillian Owens, even though it meant holding up filming while waiting for Nicole to finish her part in *Eyes Wide Shut*. By all accounts, the two stars formed a close friendship during production, despite seemingly having little in common. After filming a scene in which their characters get drunk together, Nicole and Bullock, along with Stockard Channing and Diane Wiest, decided to re-enact the scene for real, replacing the water used on set with the wine it represented.

While *Practical Magic* gathered some more praise in the press for her acting talents, and *Eyes Wide Shut* was slowly working its way through the editing stages, Nicole signed on for her next project that was a world away from what she was used to in the movies – she was to appear on the West End Stage.

Directed by Sam Mendes – later famous for winning the Oscar for Best Director for his work on the 2000 film *American Beauty*, as well as his 2003 marriage to actress Kate Winslet – Nicole was to appear in a two-hander alongside Iain Glen in which she would play five very different characters. It was to be another encounter with Arthur Schnitzler for Nicole, as this play was based on Schnitzler's work *La Ronde*. Adapted by David Hare, this production at the Donmar Warehouse was called *The Blue Room*.

Nicole was also going to work with the sexual side of Schnitzler once again, as the play covered a series of erotic encounters, some of which involved both Nicole and Glen being naked on the stage and simulating sexual intercourse. For this, both performers were being paid the Equity minimum rate of £250 a week.

Although she had performed in professional theatre before, it had been a long time since she had acted in front of a live audience, and Nicole understandably suffered from nerves before the opening night. She later admitted that she had wanted to pull out of the play, and had made a panic-stricken phone call to her father. During that call, he managed to reassure her that she could play all five characters with their different accents and she decided to give it a go.

Nicole took to the stage and wowed London's theatre critics and audiences alike. Her ability to change character and accent was applauded, as was her skill at making each incarnation believable in itself. Even the critics recognised her star-quality.

Theatrical newspaper *The Stage* also gave Nicole the seal of approval, when Peter Hepple remarked: "Nicole Kidman, the inevitable centre of attention, is not just a pretty face. She is in fact a very good actress indeed." And Charles Spencer was quoted worldwide when he said in *The Daily Telegraph*: "The vision of her wafting around the stage with a fag in one hand and her knickers in the other as a delicious French au pair will haunt my fantasies for months... Pure theatrical Viagra."

The overwhelming critical response in London sent the play to Broadway's Cort Theatre. On the other side of the Atlantic the reaction to Nicole's performance was no less enthusiastic. Nicole, however, was unable to finish the run in New York, coming down with a bronchial infection and laryngitis which forced her to withdraw 10 days before the run ended. She said in a press release that she was "truly devastated" and apologised to those who had planned to attend.

However, with the reaction she received from both audiences and critics, it is unsurprising that Nicole found herself nominated for both the Olivier and the Evening Standard Awards for Best Actress. She also won the Evening Standard Special Award.

All in all, *The Blue Room* proved both fulfiling and different professionally for Nicole. She later confirmed this, saying *"The Blue Room* was creatively the best experience I've ever had. I would go to work every day walking on air. It was just one of those things where I'd always wanted to do theatre and I was so nervous beforehand. And suddenly it was a success and I was working at this wonderful theatre."

Her appearance in the show also made her a firm friend in Iain Glen. Nicole and Cruise became patrons of Dundee Repertory Theatre in the summer of 1999, leading a campaign to fund a full-time company of actors for the venue. The theatre's artistic director was Iain Glen's brother, Hamish. A spokeswoman for Dundee Rep said: "We are thrilled that, despite their busy schedules, they were prepared to help us. Nicole started out in theatres in Australia and she recognises how important they are to communities and to the acting profession."

After a few months off, to rest, relax and get back to full health, Nicole finally got to see the final cut of *Eyes Wide Shut* at a preview with Cruise in the Spring of 1999. Astounded by what they saw, they watched it again immediately. They then rang Kubrick and Cruise passed on the message that the couple loved the film – Nicole was still resting her voice, but she faxed through a letter detailing her enthusiasm about the film. She planned to ring Kubrick later in the week – when she could speak – to tell him in person.

Sadly she would never get that chance, for that was the last contact either star would have with the famous director. Stanley Kubrick died on 7 March 1999, at the age of 70. Nicole was heartbroken that she had not had a chance to speak to him before he died, describing Kubrick as being like a father to her.

Audiences the world over waited with baited breath to see what was now Kubrick's legacy, his final finished film. Cruise and Nicole became the protectors of the film, fighting the censors every step of the way. Although the orgy scene was tampered with slightly for American audiences, those in Europe were treated to the scenes as Kubrick had wanted them shown. Upon its American release in July 1999 the film earned over $20 million on its opening weekend, shooting it straight to the top of the movie charts.

Eyes Wide Shut had its European premiere at the Venice Film Festival. Cruise and Nicole – looking refreshed and radiant – made quite an impression on the press gathered at the event, and Cruise declared that he was happy that European cinemas were to show the uncut version. Speaking of the film's late director, Cruise spoke with great pride, saying: "When we're 70 or 80-years-old, we'll look back on this century and say, 'I was there with Stanley Kubrick'."

NICOLE KIDMAN

RISING TO THE TOP

But what of the film's supposedly pornographic content? Rumours circulated wildly in the press before the film's release as to what the true nature of the so-called erotic scenes could be. BBC entertainment correspondent Tom Brook played down the sex scenes after seeing the film, saying: "It has Tom Cruise playing a far more complex character in a film which doesn't deliver as much titillating sex as the advertising suggests, or what mainstream audiences might expect." By all accounts the movie was an art house look at sexual jealousy, rather than the excuse to watch a real-life Hollywood couple's sex life as some newspapers had portrayed it.

Eyes Wide Shut contributed to Kubrick being awarded a posthumous fellowship at the BAFTAs, while Nicole received the Blockbuster Entertainment Award for Favourite Actress – Drama/Romance. Nicole and Cruise also won some more unusual accolades. Blockbuster Video customers of 2003 voted them into the top five screen lovers for *Eyes Wide Shut*, while *Heat* magazine readers in 1999 named them the sexiest couple in show business.

9

All singing and dancing

NICOLE KIDMAN

ALL SINGING AND DANCING

After spending a lot of time apart while Nicole made *Practical Magic* and appeared in *The Blue Room*, the Cruises' next projects would unite them in Sydney. Cruise was headed there to reprise his highly successful role as Ethan Hunt in *Mission: Impossible II* while Nicole was getting ready to make *Birthday Girl* which would be filmed in Australia, with outside location work later filmed in Hertfordshire, England.

Jez Butterworth was to direct *Birthday Girl*, a story about a meek man and his Russian mail-order bride, who turns out to be nothing like her description. To prepare for her role, Nicole was presented with a new challenge – she had to learn to speak Russian, as did French actors Vincent Cassel and Mathieu Kassovitz. Nicole's language coach did not let the famous actress off easily, chastising her if her accent slipped or if she didn't put quite get the right emphasis on the words. But Nicole acknowledged that she learned a lot about Russian culture as well as ensuring that she mastered a Moscow accent.

Co-star Ben Chaplin did not have to learn Russian, but he did have a lot of scenes when he was naked, including sex scenes with Nicole. Having never done such scenes before, he was understandably nervous about cavorting in the nude with a leading Hollywood actress. Nicole was quick to try and put him at his ease, although he later admitted that it was like being in a doctor's waiting room and, despite his stunning co-star, he could not wait until the scenes were over.

Birthday Girl, although filmed in late 1999, was not released until 2002, by which time Nicole had leapt to another level of fame. One of the things that helped her get there was her next project, *Moulin Rouge!* Director Baz Luhrmann – the man responsible for *Romeo & Juliet* with Leonardo DiCaprio and Claire Danes – had personally courted

ALL SINGING AND DANCING

Nicole to play the role of doomed courtesan Satine, sending her flowers while she was appearing in *The Blue Room* with an intriguing card that read: "I have this great character. She sings, she dances, and then she dies."

Luhrmann's reworking of the Orpheus in the underworld myth sees Christian (played by Ewan McGregor) descending into the underworld of the Moulin Rouge, falling in love with a courtesan and trying to rescue his new love from her situation. What Luhrmann also added to the plot was pop music – the characters sing songs ranging from Madonna's *Like a Virgin* to Police's *Roxanne* and Elton John's *Your Song*.

Once again Nicole found herself suffering from last minute nerves. "I called up Baz before we started", she later admitted, "and said, 'I think you're going to have to recast it because there's no way my voice is going to be good enough, I can't do the role and you've made a big mistake.'" Fortunately, he didn't believe her.

Four months of rehearsals in Sydney enabled the cast to get to know each other. As well as Nicole and McGregor, *Moulin Rouge!* also featured performers such as John Leguizamo, Jim Broadbent and Richard Roxburgh. Any embarrassment was

ALL SINGING AND DANCING

pushed aside as the actors sang and danced in front of one another, preparing themselves as much as they could for an exhausting shoot.

It did not begin well, when Baz Luhrmann's father died on the first day of filming. The director later admitted that he was emotionally absent for the first few weeks of production, but the cast worked hard and pulled together. Nicole found inspiration from women such as Rita Hayworth, Cyd Charisse, Ginger Rogers and Marlene Dietrich – and that element of old Hollywood is very much in evidence in her performance.

She also enjoyed working with Ewan McGregor, whose previous appearances in films such as *Trainspotting* and *Star Wars Episode I – The Phantom Menace* had probably not prepared him for an all-singing, all-dancing romantic lead role. "From the moment we met we just hit it off," said Nicole of her co-star. Although the story of Moulin Rouge was a tragic one, by all accounts there were a lot of laughs during production between performers.

But filming was not going to be an easy experience for Nicole, however much fun she was having with her co-stars between takes. First she snapped a rib performing ballet lifts. Production was shut down for two weeks while she recovered. As soon as she was put back into her corset costume her rib snapped again, and another two weeks production was lost. In the last fortnight of production she fell in her high heels and tore the cartilage behind her kneecap. This time, with the finish date in sight, Nicole worked through the pain.

When production on *Moulin Rouge!* ended, Nicole was exhausted and thought she'd had enough of movies. But there was no way Nicole was not going to work again. In fact she began filming *The Others* in September 2000.

The Others was to be directed by the young Chilean Alejandro Amenábar, whose previous works *Tesis* and *Abre Los Ojos* were both in Spanish. The ghost story with a difference was to be his first movie in English, and with Nicole as the star and Cruise stepping in as executive producer, Amenábar could not have asked for a better introduction to Hollywood.

Nicole, who originally had doubts about the content of the film, was later to praise her young director in *The Washington Diplomat*, saying: "He has an incredible ability to build true suspense, which comes from the heart and mind, from the inside rather than the outside."

NICOLE KIDMAN

ALL SINGING AND DANCING

Amenábar said of Nicole: "It was an incredible experience working with her. It was a daily challenge because Nicole is very demanding (a perfectionist) and professional. As a director I tried my best to create the perfect atmosphere for her to be able to create her character."

Filming was completed on *The Others* in December 2000, the same month the Cruises celebrated their 10th wedding anniversary. Nicole was looking ahead to 2001, with both *Moulin Rouge!* and *The Others* due for release, she was also getting ready to start filming *The Hours*. As late as December 2000, Nicole Kidman could still have been thinking that 2001 was going to be a great year for her.

NICOLE KIDMAN

ALL SINGING AND DANCING

Spotlight on... the *Moulin Rouge!* team

All films are a product of team-work. However, musicals are often more reliant on a talented ensemble cast than other genres. *Moulin Rouge!* enjoyed great success, not only because of Nicole's star turn as Satine, but also because of those who surrounded her.

Australian director Baz Luhrmann – who also has a co-writing credit for *Moulin Rouge!* – had quite a reputation before making the film, despite having only two previous movies to his credit.

Strictly Ballroom was made in 1992 and was inspired by Luhrmann's parents' participation in ballroom competitions. Although not as luscious as *Moulin Rouge!*, this story of two misfits proving themselves in the Australian ballroom dancing championships is still visually stunning, with bright bold colours. *Romeo & Juliet* elaborated on Luhrmann's style and also featured swift cut-away shots and a star-studded cast including Leonardo DiCaprio and Clare Danes.

Luhrmann also produced and directed a version of the opera *La Boheme* for the Sydney stage. His version of the opera, which took place in Paris in the Fifties, was later filmed and screened on television. Another of Luhrmann's projects was the music single *Everybody's Free (To Wear Sunscreen)* which was released in 1999. Although Luhrmann's name was on the single, his role was a producing one, the song – a series of advice tips spoken over music – was written by *Chicago Tribune* journalist Mary Schmich and performed by Lee Perry.

Strictly Ballroom and *Romeo & Juliet*, along with *Moulin Rouge!* are known in film circles as Luhrmann's Red Curtain Trilogy as all employ the same sumptuous style of film-making. Next he plans on making a set of three historical films, the first of which is an as-yet-untitled project about the life of Alexander the Great starring Nicole and Leonardo DiCaprio.

Nicole's *Moulin Rouge!* co-star Ewan McGregor, born and bred in Scotland, started his career on British television in the Channel 4 series *Lipstick on Your Collar.* By the time *Moulin Rouge!* began filming McGregor was enjoying a successful career, with British films such as *Trainspotting*, *Brassed Off* and *Little Voice* to his name. However, it was his appearance as Obi-Wan Kenobi in *Star Wars Episode I - The Phantom Menace* in 1999 that made his a household name on both sides of the Atlantic.

NICOLE KIDMAN

ALL SINGING AND DANCING

When Channel 4 released their 100 Greatest Movie Stars, McGregor was ranked number nine.

Although there were rumours linking Nicole to McGregor during the filming of *Moulin Rouge!*, they could not have been further from the truth. Although the co-stars did get on very well, McGregor is happily married to Eve Mavrakis, whom he met when working on television show *Kavanagh QC* in 1994. They married a year later and have two daughters, Clara Mathilde and Esther Rose.

McGregor was not the only talented Brit on the *Moulin Rouge!* set. Englishman Jim Broadbent played Harold Zidler, coming to the set straight after finishing his role in *Bridget Jones's Diary*. Known for his role as DCI Roy Slater in *Only Fools and Horses*, Broadbent also appeared alongside McGregor in *Little Voice* and brought a respected career of character acting to the *Moulin Rouge!* set.

And there was another famous Australian, besides Nicole, making an appearance in *Moulin Rouge!* Although Kylie Minogue began her career as an actress on Australian television shows such as *The Sullivans*, *Skyways*, *The Henderson Kids* and *Neighbours*, she had become far more famous as a pop singer. Although her film experience was patchy, she was perfect for the role of the Green Fairy, standing at a petite 5'1" and sporting a perfect figure.

Playing Henri Toulouse-Lautrec, John Leguizamo had worked with Luhrmann before when he played Tybalt in *Romeo & Juliet*. He was also no stranger to unusual roles, having played Miss Chi-Chi Rodriguez in *To Wong Foo, Thanks for Everything! Julie Newmar* in 1995 and the voice of a rat in the 1998 remake of *Doctor Dolittle*.

Richard Roxburgh – who plays The Duke – is another Australian. He has recently appeared as Count Dracula in *Van Helsing* and M in *The League of Extraordinary Gentlemen*, so is still enjoying being good at being bad. He also starred alongside Tom Cruise in *Mission: Impossible II*.

10

Going solo

NICOLE KIDMAN

GOING SOLO

On 4 February 2001, Tom Cruise packed his bags and left the family home in Pacific Palisades, moving into the Bel-Air Hotel. The next day his representative released the following statement to the press: "Tom Cruise and Nicole Kidman announced today that they have regretfully decided to separate. The couple, who married in 1990, stressed their great respect for each other both personally and professionally. Citing the difficulties inherent in divergent careers which constantly kept them apart, they concluded that an amicable separation seemed best for both of them at this time."

GOING SOLO

Although it is unclear how much of a surprise this development was to Nicole, what is certain is that it shook her world to the core. The media went crazy. Although the couple had obviously had some problems in private, their marriage had been seen as one of Hollywood's most stable, passing the 10-year mark in a town famous for quickie marriages and equally quick divorces. The cinematic releases of both *Moulin Rouge!* and *The Others* were put on hold until Nicole felt ready for the necessary publicity tours.

Although Nicole originally hoped for a reconciliation, Cruise did not seem interested. The day after the separation statement was read to the press, Cruise filed for divorce citing irreconcilable differences. What was an issue for debate, however, was the length of time the couple had been married. Cruise was claiming that they had decided to separate 72 hours before their 10th wedding anniversary, an important distinction under Californian law.

Nicole kept quiet at the time, releasing only a brief statement to the press stating that the divorce was not her idea, however, she debated the timing of their separation when it came to filing court papers, which read: "On 24 December the parties had happily celebrated their 10th anniversary with a group of friends. During the balance of December and thereafter the parties were intimate."

At this time Nicole's female support system rallied around her. Mother Janelle and sister Antonia flew in from Australia and Naomi Watts was always there for her.

Sadly, despite being surrounded by those who cared for her, Nicole's year was not going to get any better. In March she discovered the shattering news that she had been pregnant, but had lost the baby shortly before the three-month mark. Speaking of that time, Nicole would later say, "it was dark and deeply lonely". She then had the unenviable task of contacting her estranged husband and letting him know what had happened to his baby, before he read about it in the papers.

That same month Nicole also endured the attentions of a stalker who plied her with poetry and set up a website that was eventually used in court to demonstrate his extreme fanaticism. Nicole managed to get a restraining order after the man had threatened her staff with violence when they refused to let him into her home. Speaking about it later that year, she gave her opinion of the time. "In the weirdest way it has opened me up," she said, "I have carried the thought with me that whatever happens in the future, it won't get much worse than this."

Although she was able to look back and feel stronger, Nicole also admitted that, at the time, she just crawled into bed and stayed there for days, unable to face the world. As if the divorce and miscarriage were not enough, she also had to deal with rumours in the press concerning the nature of Cruise's relationship with his *Vanilla Sky* co-star Penelope Cruz, as well as the intense media interest in her private business. She escaped to Sydney for a while.

However, her time Down Under was not to be long, and she returned to America to do what she did best – work. Shortly before her break-up with Cruise, the knee that Nicole had injured while making *Moulin Rouge!* had forced her to drop out of making *Panic Room* with director David Fincher. She was replaced by Jodie Foster in the drama about a woman and her daughter trapped in their own house as intruders search for the concealed room in which they are hiding.

Nicole admitted later that she was devastated to have to drop out of *Panic Room* after three weeks of shooting, but she was physically weak at the

GOING SOLO

time – despite her belief she could continue working, her body had other ideas. Rumour has it, however, that Nicole did not disappear from *Panic Room* entirely, still playing a small role as a voice on the other end of the telephone.

Not quite ready to get back on to a film set, Nicole instead hit the publicity trail. *Moulin Rouge!* opened the Cannes Film Festival, and Nicole drafted in her sister Antonia as her date for the big event. The film was a smash hit, entrancing audiences with a style of musical that had never been seen before. As Nicole promoted the film, rumours began linking her with her co-star Ewan McGregor. Ridiculous as these ideas were – McGregor was a happily married man – this was something that the newly single Nicole was going to be a victim of more and more, until she herself put a stop to it in the courtroom.

Moulin Rouge! was also a hit when awards time rolled around. Nicole was nominated for the Best Actress Oscar, but lost out to Halle Berry's powerful performance in *Monster's Ball*. Still Nicole literally shone at the ceremony, wearing Chanel couture – a layered pink chiffon creation by Karl Lagerfield – accessorised by a $4 million Bulgari diamond choker. Once again, Antonia was her date.

NICOLE KIDMAN

GOING SOLO

Awards-wise, she was more successful elsewhere, picking up the prize at the Golden Globes, the Empire Awards and the MTV Movie Awards.

Although *The Others* and *Birthday Girl* were yet to be released, Nicole now considered herself ready to start work on a new project – *The Hours*. Director Stephen Daldry had already been shooting the film since early 2001, however due to the movie's split nature, Nicole was not needed until the summer of that year. Back in England for location work in Richmond-on-Thames, Nicole donned a prosthetic nose and dowdy clothes as she became almost unrecognisable as Virginia Woolf. She enjoyed the freedom this change in appearance gave her, sometimes laughing at the photographers who lurked for a picture of Nicole Kidman, never realising how close they were to her.

Away from the film set, Cruise had come out and confirmed that he and Penelope Cruz had been seeing one another romantically. The new couple had met on the set of *Vanilla Sky*, a remake of Alejandro Amenábar's *Aber Los Ojos* in which Cruz had also starred. A native of Madrid, she also had several important American films under her belt before meeting Cruise, including *All the Pretty Horses*, *Blow* and *Captain Corelli's Mandolin*. Now their relationship was out in open, Cruz knew she would be compared to Nicole. However, all she would say publicly was: "I have huge respect for Nicole Kidman and I think she is one of the best actresses working right now."

This news certainly affected the plans for a family holiday that Cruise and Nicole had made in happier times. They agreed to split the two-week break in Fiji between them. Nicole would take the first week with the children and Cruise the second, along with his new girlfriend. However, it was Nicole's love life that would be the focus of the press rumours when it was reported that she was visited in Fiji by Russell Crowe.

Although Crowe was reportedly accompanied by a female companion, it did not stop the media speculation concerning a possible romance between the two old friends. Crowe seemed to find the whole episode extremely amusing when he made the situation clear to the press. He assured reporters that he and Nicole were good friends, but that there was no romance between them. Indeed Nicole Kidman was rumoured to be on the guest list when Crowe wed long-term girlfriend Danielle Spencer in April 2003.

In an attempt to quash any more romantic

rumours before they started, Nicole's dates for the premiere of *The Others* were Naomi Watts and a heavily pregnant Rebecca Rigg, whose baby Harry is now Nicole's godson. She towered over her friends in her rediscovered high-heeled shoes, something she could wear to her heart's content after her split with Cruise – she also famously exclaimed "I can wear heels now!" on *The David Letterman Show*. The potential for awkwardness was there at the premiere, as both Nicole and Cruise were attending. However, as was remarked upon in the press, the pair managed to avoid bumping into each other.

Just days after the premiere of *The Others*, Nicole and Cruise's fast-track divorce was finalised. Neither was present in court. All money arrangements were decided between them a couple of months later, with the details remaining private.

Nicole was ready to try something new, and she got the opportunity when Robbie Williams approached her to duet with him on a rerecording of the Frank and Nancy Sinatra classic *Somethin' Stupid*. Williams had heard a copy of the *Moulin Rouge!* soundtrack and proclaimed himself "thrilled" that such a big Hollywood star would agree to work with him.

After recording the song in the same studio that Sinatra had once worked in, Williams decided to release the song as a Christmas single. This meant a video had to be recorded. While Nicole and Williams worked on the video, the press followed them around, hoping that there was a romance between the two celebrities.

Williams is famous for his cheeky, cocky persona. He enjoys taking the press for a ride and it is likely that this is what was happening when he made his statements about his feelings for Nicole. Although the video for *Somethin' Stupid* was deliberately sexy, with both performers stripping down to just their jewellery, Nicole laughingly denied all rumours of an affair. "Me and Robbie?" she said. "My God, are you mad? He's so funny, we wouldn't be able to stop giggling long enough to have sex!"

There may not have been any relationship, but there was a friendship that provided Nicole with some laughs, something she certainly needed that year. The single went to number one on the UK charts and Nicole later attended Williams' concert in Sydney, dancing in the aisles like any other fan. However, the whole rumoured romance

GOING SOLO

once again made Nicole aware of the media interest in her love life. "It is hard to make friends when you can't just do anything or go anywhere because people are constantly watching you," she told *Vogue* magazine. Nicole was also linked around this time with Adam Duritz, the lead singer of Counting Crows around this time. This was one of the more bizarre rumours, as Nicole had not even met Duritz.

But laughs and relationship rumours aside, it was time for Nicole to get back to making movies. Her first project was one she had considered appearing in, but decided that she would rather produce. Directed by Jane Campion, *In the Cut* starred Meg Ryan, stepping out of her girl-next-door roles to play a woman who searches for and embarks on a dangerous sexual affair. Based on the novel by Susanna Moore, Nicole had acquired the screen rights with Jane Campion back in 1996. Campion, who directed the film, originally wanted Nicole for the part, but she was to be tied up – literally – elsewhere.

Nicole's next acting project was going to be directed by the controversial Lars von Trier, who had also directed 2000's *Dancer in the Dark* with Icelandic singer Björk. Called *Dogville*, the film was shot in Sweden despite being set in America. Not that the location mattered, as the film was shot in a studio and it had no props. The town was indicated by chalk marks on the floor.

Nicole explains Von Trier's vision of her, saying: "We wanted to make a film where you take the walls away in society and how you can actually see everybody doing their business as if they were in town. The dog in the film is actually the chalk mark, and we all sort of go and pat the dog – but the dog is just a chalk mark. It's either going to work or it's going to be a disaster."

With a supporting cast that included Lauren Bacall and James Caan, the plot of *Dogville* involves Nicole's character Grace – said to have been written by Lars von Trier especially for her – taking refuge in a small town while on the run from the mob. However, the people of Dogville have their price for protecting Grace, while she in turn has a secret of her own. There was a harrowing rape scene for Nicole to endure, as well as the scenes where the women seek to punish her. Many wondered why Nicole put herself through an experience like this for little money, when she could be starring in blockbusters. She explained that she preferred doing experimental things.

NICOLE KIDMAN

GOING SOLO

Although *Dogville* cannot have been easy to film, Nicole turns in a great performance, and the movie was nominated for the illustrious Palm d'Or at the Cannes Film Festival. Nicole did not stop to enjoy her success, however, moving straight on to her next film, *The Human Stain.*

Directed by Robert Benton – who had been so encouraging back when he directed her in *Billy Bathgate* – and co-starring Anthony Hopkins and Ed Harris, *The Human Stain* is based on the novel by Philip Roth. Hopkins plays a college professor who has many secrets that are all revealed over the course of the film. One of the secrets is his affair with Nicole's character. The 29-year-age-gap between Nicole and Hopkins was remarked upon in the press, but worked well on-screen.

So, although 2001 started badly for Nicole, she pushed through the pain with support from family and friends, and work – which always seems to help her cope with things. And all the hard work paid off. Not only did she win the Best Actress Oscar for *The Hours*, but she also won the Golden Globe for the second year running as well as the BAFTA for Best Actress in a Leading Role. She proved herself with difficult performances in unusual films, as well as tackling a musical and coming out on top with her first run at the pop charts.

But Nicole does not pretend her life is perfect. She had always wanted the kind of relationship her parents enjoyed and had hoped to raise her children in a similar, safe 'cocoon', but by acknowledging that things are difficult for her, she has won over a new set of fans.

She may have still been fighting, but Nicole was certainly winning the battle. She had survived the worst year of her life. There was no stopping her now.

11

A bright future

NICOLE KIDMAN

A BRIGHT FUTURE

After her Oscar triumph, there was an increased focus on Nicole's films. The public and the media held high expectations of her as an actress, and Nicole was anxious not to disappoint.

Cold Mountain once again proved her acting talents, casting her alongside Jude Law and Renée Zellweger in the American Civil War tale of a Confederate soldier who is wounded and trying to make his way back to Ada, the woman he left behind. Meanwhile Ada – played by Nicole – is trying to cope on her father's farm, where she is helped by Ruby (Zellweger, in Oscar-winning form).

After her roles in *The Hours* and *Dogville,*

NICOLE KIDMAN

A BRIGHT FUTURE

Nicole loved her part in *Cold Mountain*. She felt that Ada's character was about hope and people helping each other in times of need. She drew strength from her kindness.

Although the film was set in North Carolina, and some of it was shot there, budgetary constraints meant that a lot of scenes were filmed in the Romanian town of Potigrafu. Director Anthony Minghella – whose previous work included *The English Patient* and *The Talented Mr Ripley* was devastated that filming couldn't happen in North Carolina. Although once discovering the landscape of Romania he felt that it made the film beautiful.

As Ada, Nicole developed her character from a delicate woman at the beginning to a strong farmworker by the end. She described this development as "one of the most powerful parts of the film" and one of the main reasons she wanted to take the part. "Also, I wanted to work with Renee," Nicole added. "I thought the two of us up a mountain together would become fun."

Although Nicole was roundly praised by the critics for her gritty performance, she was disappointed at Oscar time when she did not receive a nomination, despite many pundits predicting her

A BRIGHT FUTURE

as a second-time winner. But *Cold Mountain* would not leave Nicole without recognition – she was nominated for both the Golden Globe and the Empire Award for Best Actress. In 2003 Nicole was also finally presented with her own star on the Hollywood Walk of Fame – exactly a decade after accompanying Tom Cruise to his ceremony. She joked at the time: "I've never been so excited to have people walk all over me for the rest of my life! I love to act and this is sort of the icing on the cake." Nicole was also presented with an American Cinematheque Award at a Gala Tribute in the same year.

However, Nicole's lack of an Oscar nomination was not the only gossip surrounding the *Cold Mountain* release. Rumours swirled around the media during the filming and promotional periods of the film that Nicole and her on-screen romance Jude Law were getting very close. This was truly titillating gossip, considering that Law was thought at the time to be happily married to Sadie Frost, with whom he has three children.

Although the marriage between Law and Frost was in trouble at this stage, and the pair divorced in October 2003, there was no confirmation that the rumours concerning a relationship between

A BRIGHT FUTURE

Nicole and Law were true. When the troubles in his marriage were made public, Law spoke out about how there was "absolutely no third party involved" in their problems. At the premiere for *The Hours* the press fired questions about Law at Nicole, which she politely answered, denying any affair.

But it seems that Nicole could only be pushed so far. She had been forced to put up with ridiculous rumours concerning her love life since her split with Cruise – rumours had her linked with George Clooney, Russell Crowe, Robbie Williams and Adam Duritz to name but a few. And when *The Sun* published an article that stated as fact the alleged affair between her and Jude Law, Nicole had finally had enough.

In October 2003 she took the paper to court and won undisclosed libel damages – believed to be a five-figure amount – and an apology from *The Sun*. Her lawyer Keith Schilling said in court that "the publication of the article caused damage to the claimant's personal and professional reputation and she has suffered considerable embarrassment and distress". Nicole donated her damages balance to a charity which looks after abandoned children in Romania, the location of some of the shooting on *Cold Mountain*.

NICOLE KIDMAN

A BRIGHT FUTURE

Unlike the whole business with Jude Law, claims in the media that Nicole was seeing rocker Lenny Kravitz were not met with such denial, with Nicole's spokeswoman Leslie Dart telling *People* magazine: "They're very close. He's very important to her." Kravitz – who has enjoyed chart success with his album *Are You Gonna Go My Way* and singles *American Woman*, *Fly Away* and *It Ain't Over 'Til It's Over* – is also divorced with a child. Although the pair were seen in each other's company a lot during late 2003, Nicole has forced the media to focus on her work rather than her private life. She refuses to speak about personal matters and turns in constantly convincing performances that even the gossip-hungry press cannot ignore.

Coming up next at cinemas is *Birth*, in which Nicole plays a woman who is convinced that a young boy is her dead husband reincarnated. Co-starring Anne Heche and Lauren Bacall, the film is directed by Jonathan Glazer.

Following on from *Birth* will be a comedy remake of the 1975 sci-fi cult movie *The Stepford Wives*, with Nicole taking the role of Joanna Eberhart that was played by Katharine Ross in the original. The plot concerns a couple who move to a small town and discover that the men are murdering

A BRIGHT FUTURE

their wives and replacing them with sexy robot slaves who love looking after their husbands. When Joanna Eberhart's husband Walter, played by Matthew Broderick, begins to think this is a good idea, Joanna has to fight for her life.

Directed by Frank Oz, *The Stepford Wives* will also star Bette Midler, Christopher Walken, Faith Hill and Glenn Close. Having made a lot of serious films preceding this one, Nicole was initially relieved at the lighter subject matter, until she realised that playing it for laughs was not as easy as it looked. "I have just finished *The Stepford Wives*, which we hope is a comedy," she said. "I tell you, comedy is a lot harder. I was exhausted when I finished that."

Back in a more serious frame of mind, Nicole is also going to play a translator whose life is put in danger when she overhears a conversation about the death of an African leader. Directed by Sydney Pollack and co-starring Sean Penn, *The Interpreter* has already made a little bit of movie history by being the first film to get permission to film inside the United Nations building. The makers of other movies – including Nicole's previous work *The Peacemaker* – had to settle for filming outside the building. Nicole also prepared

A BRIGHT FUTURE

for the role by attending a Security Council meeting on Iraq and watching the translators at work.

Other projects are always being rumoured and hinted at. An as-yet-untitled film about Alexander the Great is said to be in production, starring Leonardo DiCaprio as Alexander and Nicole as Olympias. Directed by *Moulin Rouge!*'s Baz Luhrmann – who has also worked previously with DiCaprio on *Romeo & Juliet* – this would be another high-profile historical film for Nicole's CV.

Another remake is also rumoured to be in pre-production, this time of the classic Sixties television show *Bewitched.* Playing the role of beautiful witch Samantha Stephens would be a bonus for Nicole, as she is a fan of the actress Elizabeth Montgomery, who played the original Samantha.

Will Ferrell is slated to play Samantha's long-suffering husband Darrin, while Shirley MacLaine and Michael Caine are expected to play Endora and Maurice respectively. Written and directed by Nora Ephron – who was the talent behind *Sleepless in Seattle* and *You've Got Mail* – *Bewitched* would be another lightweight film for Nicole to enjoy making.

After her brilliant performance in *Moulin Rouge!* it is not surprising that Nicole is expected to appear in two more musicals. The first is a

A BRIGHT FUTURE

remake of *The Producers* – the 1968 film written and directed by Mel Brooks, which went on to be a smash hit Broadway show starring Matthew Broderick and Nathan Lane. Both Broderick and Lane are expected to reprise their roles for the film, and Nicole is said to be playing Ulla (originally played by Lee Meredith) in the Susan Stroman-directed remake.

Details are rather more sketchy for the second musical, *American Darlings*. Set in the Second World War and telling the story of female swing musicians battling it out to be allowed to play alongside the men, and a rumour that it is to co-star singer and actress Jennifer Lopez has caught the press's attention.

Also announced, but still very light on the details, is a possible project *Emma's War*, based on Deborah Scroggin's book about a British aid worker who marries a warlord. Direction is rumoured to be by Tony Scott – whom Nicole worked with on *Days of Thunder*, and who is also responsible for *Enemy of the State*, *True Romance* and *Top Gun*.

What is evident is Nicole is going to be appearing on our screens for some time to come. She has certainly come a long way from the amateur theatres of Sydney, and from the

NICOLE KIDMAN

A BRIGHT FUTURE

Hollywood wife of a superstar. However, she still hates watching herself.

Recently Australia's *Business Review Weekly* publication placed Nicole as Australia's richest entertainer, estimating she earned £10.3 million in 2003. Nicole's good friend Russell Crowe was placed fourth, and the article pointed out: "Australian entertainers are at the top of their game. Nicole Kidman and Russell Crowe are arguably the world's most prominent actors." The article also estimated Nicole's worth at around £90 million and discussed her homes in Sydney, California, New York and London.

Nicole also topped another poll in 2004, when she was voted favourite movie star waxwork by the visitors at Madame Tussaud's, London – beating tough competition from Renee Zellweger and Julia Roberts.

Since beginning her career at such a young age, Nicole has been recognised as a beautiful woman with an extraordinary talent. She is also highly regarded for her fashion sense and is one of the most photographed women at awards ceremonies or premieres. And although she may be an internationally renowned movie star, at home she is mother to Conor and Isabella, a job

A BRIGHT FUTURE

she thoroughly enjoys.

When asked to summarise her career, Nicole answered in a typically honest fashion. "In the end", she said, "I hope I've done some unusual films and tried to keep my very public life private, quiet and dignified." Although the press have not made this easy for her, Nicole has certainly kept her family life as private as possible while making a success of a varied film career that few actresses would attempt, let alone pull off with such style.

12

Filmography

NICOLE KIDMAN

FILMOGRAPHY

Bush Christmas (1983)
Helen
BMX Bandits (1983)
Judy
Wills & Burke (1985)
Julia Matthews
Archer's Adventure (1985)
Catherine
Windrider (1986)
Jade
Watch the Shadows Dance (1987)
Amy Gabriel
The Bit Part (1987)
Mary McAllister
Emerald City (1988)
Helen, Mike McCord's Girlfriend
Dead Calm (1989)
Rae Ingram
Days of Thunder (1990)
Dr Claire Lewicki
Flirting (1991)
Nicola
Billy Bathgate (1991)
Drew Preston
Far and Away (1992)
Shannon Christie

NICOLE KIDMAN

FILMOGRAPHY

Malice (1993)
Tracy Kennsinger
My Life (1993)
Gail Jones
To Die For (1995)
Suzanne Stone-Maretto
Batman Forever (1995)
Dr Chase Meridian
The Leading Man (1996)
Academy Awards Presenter
The Portrait of a Lady (1996)
Isabel Archer
The Peacemaker (1997)
Dr Julia Kelly
Practical Magic (1998)
Gillian Owens
Eyes Wide Shut (1999)
Alice Harford
Moulin Rouge! (2001)
Satine
The Others (2001)
Grace
Birthday Girl (2001)
Sophia
The Hours (2002)
Virginia Woolf

NICOLE KIDMAN

FILMOGRAPHY

Dogville (2003)
Grace
The Human Stain (2003)
Faunia Farley
Cold Mountain (2003)
Ada Monroe

UPCOMING RELEASES

The Interpreter
The Stepford Wives
Birth

BIOGRAPHIES

OTHER BOOKS IN THE SERIES

Also available in the series:

OTHER BOOKS IN THE SERIES

JENNIFER ANISTON

She's been a Friend to countless millions worldwide, and overcame numerous hurdles to rise to the very top of her field. From a shy girl with a dream of being a famous actress, through being reduced to painting scenery for high school plays, appearing in a series of flop TV shows and one rather bad movie, Jennifer Aniston has persevered, finally finding success at the very top of the TV tree.

Bringing the same determination that got her a part on the world's best-loved TV series to her attempts at a film career, she's also worked her way from rom-com cutie up to serious, respected actress and box office draw, intelligently combining indie, cult and comedy movies into a blossoming career which looks set to shoot her to the heights of Hollywood's A-list. She's also found love with one of the world's most desirable men. Is Jennifer Aniston the ultimate Hollywood Renaissance woman? It would seem she's got more than a shot at such a title, as indeed, she seems to have it all, even if things weren't always that way. Learn all about Aniston's rise to fame in this compelling biography.

OTHER BOOKS IN THE SERIES

DAVID BECKHAM

This book covers the amazing life of the boy from East London who has not only become a world class footballer and the captain of England, but also an idol to millions, and probably the most famous man in Britain.

His biography tracks his journey, from the playing fields of Chingford to the Bernabau. It examines how he joined his beloved Manchester United and became part of a golden generation of talent that led to United winning trophies galore.

Beckham's parallel personal life is also examined, as he moved from tongue-tied football-obsessed kid to suitor of a Spice Girl, to one half of Posh & Becks, the most famous celebrity couple in Britain – perhaps the world. His non-footballing activities, his personal indulgences and changing styles have invited criticism, and even abuse, but his football talent has confounded the critics, again and again.

The biography looks at his rise to fame and his relationship with Posh, as well as his decision to leave Manchester for Madrid. Has it affected his relationship with Posh? What will the latest controversy over his sex life mean for celebrity's royal couple? And will he come back to play in England again?

OTHER BOOKS IN THE SERIES

GEORGE CLOONEY

The tale of George Clooney's astonishing career is an epic every bit as riveting as one of his blockbuster movies. It's a story of tenacity and determination, of fame and infamy, a story of succeeding on your own terms regardless of the risks. It's also a story of emergency rooms, batsuits, tidal waves and killer tomatoes, but let's not get ahead of ourselves.

Born into a family that, by Sixties' Kentucky standards, was dripping with show business glamour, George grew up seeing the hard work and heartache that accompanied a life in the media spotlight.

By the time stardom came knocking for George Clooney, it found a level-headed and mature actor ready and willing to embrace the limelight, while still indulging a lifelong love of partying and practical jokes. A staunchly loyal friend and son, a bachelor with a taste for the high life, a vocal activist for the things he believes and a born and bred gentleman; through failed sitcoms and blockbuster disasters, through artistic credibility and box office success, George Clooney has remained all of these things...and much, much more. Prepare to meet Hollywood's most fascinating megastar in this riveting biography.

OTHER BOOKS IN THE SERIES

BILLY CONNOLLY

In a 2003 London Comedy Poll to find Britain's favourite comedian, Billy Connolly came out on top. It's more than just Billy Connolly's all-round comic genius that puts him head and shoulders above the rest. Connolly has also proved himself to be an accomplished actor with dozens of small and big screen roles to his name. In 2003, he could be seen in *The Last Samurai* with Tom Cruise.

Connolly has also cut the mustard in the USA, 'breaking' that market in a way that chart-topping pop groups since The Beatles and the Stones have invariably failed to do, let alone mere stand-up comedians. Of course, like The Beatles and the Stones, Billy Connolly has been to the top of the pop charts too with D.I.V.O.R.C.E. in 1975.

On the way he's experienced heartache of his own with a difficult childhood and a divorce of his own, found the time and energy to bring up five children, been hounded by the press on more than one occasion, and faced up to some considerable inner demons. But Billy Connolly is a survivor. Now in his 60s, he's been in show business for all of 40 years, and 2004 finds him still touring. This exciting biography tells the story an extraordinary entertainer.

OTHER BOOKS IN THE SERIES

ROBERT DE NIRO

Robert De Niro is cinema's greatest chameleon. Snarling one minute, smirking the next, he's straddled Hollywood for a quarter of a century, making his name as a serious character actor, in roles ranging from psychotic taxi drivers to hardened mobsters. The scowls and pent-up violence may have won De Niro early acclaim but, ingeniously, he's now playing them for laughs, poking fun at the tough guy image he so carefully cultivated. Ever the perfectionist, De Niro holds nothing back on screen, but in real life he is a very private man – he thinks of himself as just another guy doing a job. Some job, some guy. There's more to the man than just movies. De Niro helped New York pick itself up after the September 11 terrorist attacks on the Twin Towers by launching the TriBeCa Film Festival and inviting everyone downtown. He runs several top-class restaurants and has dated some of the most beautiful women in the world, least of all supermodel Naomi Campbell. Now in his 60s, showered with awards and a living legend, De Niro's still got his foot on the pedal. There are six, yes six, films coming your way in 2004. In this latest biography, you'll discover all about his latest roles and the life of this extraordinary man.

OTHER BOOKS IN THE SERIES

MICHAEL DOUGLAS

Douglas may have been a shaggy-haired member of a hippy commune in the Sixties but just like all the best laidback, free-loving beatniks, he's gone on to blaze a formidable career, in both acting and producing.

In a career that has spanned nearly 40 years so far, Douglas has produced a multitude of hit movies including the classic *One Flew Over The Cuckoo's Nest* and *The China Syndrome* through to box office smashes such as *Starman* and *Face/Off*.

His acting career has been equally successful – from *Romancing The Stone* to *Wall Street* to *Fatal Attraction*, Douglas's roles have shown that he isn't afraid of putting himself on the line when up there on the big screen.

His relationship with his father; his stay in a top clinic to combat his drinking problem; the breakdown of his first marriage; and his publicised clash with the British media have all compounded to create the image of a man who's transformed himself from being the son of Hollywood legend Kirk Douglas, into Kirk Douglas being the dad of Hollywood legend, Michael Douglas.

OTHER BOOKS IN THE SERIES

HUGH GRANT

He's the Oxford fellow who stumbled into acting, the middle-class son of a carpet salesman who became famous for bumbling around stately homes and posh weddings. The megastar actor who claims he doesn't like acting, but has appeared in over 40 movies and TV shows.

On screen he's romanced a glittering array of Hollywood's hottest actresses, and tackled medical conspiracies and the mafia. Off screen he's hogged the headlines with his high profile girlfriend as well as finding lifelong notoriety after a little Divine intervention in Los Angeles.

Hugh Grant is Britain's biggest movie star, an actor whose talent for comedy has often been misjudged by those who assume he simply plays himself.

From bit parts in Nottingham theatre, through comedy revues at the Edinburgh Fringe, and on to the top of the box office charts, Hugh has remained constant – charming, witty and ever so slightly sarcastic, obsessed with perfection and performance while winking to his audience as if to say: "This is all awfully silly, isn't it?" Don't miss this riveting biography.

OTHER BOOKS IN THE SERIES

MICHAEL JACKSON

Friday 29 August 1958 was not a special day in Gary, Indiana, and indeed Gary, was far from being a special place. But it was on this day and in this location that the world's greatest entertainer was to be born, Michael Joseph Jackson.

The impact that this boy was destined to have on the world of entertainment could never have been estimated. Here we celebrate Michael Jackson's extraordinary talents, and plot the defining events over his 40-year career. This biography explores the man behind the myth, and gives an understanding of what drives this special entertainer.

In 1993, there was an event that was to rock Jackson's world. His friendship with a 12-year-old boy and the subsequent allegations resulted in a lawsuit, a fall in record sales and a long road to recovery. Two marriages, three children and 10 years later there is a feeling of déjà vu as Jackson again deals with more controversy. Without doubt, 2004 proves to be the most important year in the singer's life. Whatever that future holds for Jackson, his past is secured, there has never been and there will never again be anything quite like Michael Jackson.

OTHER BOOKS IN THE SERIES

JENNIFER LOPEZ

There was no suggestion that the Jennifer Lopez of the early Nineties would become the accomplished actress, singer and icon that she is today. Back then she was a dancer on the popular comedy show *In Living Color* – one of the Fly Girls, the accompaniment, not the main event. In the early days she truly was Jenny from the block; the Bronx native of Puerto Rican descent – another hopeful from the east coast pursuing her dreams in the west.

Today, with two marriages under her belt, three multi-platinum selling albums behind her and an Oscar-winning hunk as one of her ex-boyfriends, she is one of the most talked about celebrities of the day. Jennifer Lopez is one of the most celebrated Hispanic actresses of all time.

Her beauty, body and famous behind, are lusted after by men and envied by women throughout the world. She has proven that she can sing, dance and act. Yet her critics dismiss her as a diva without talent. And the criticisms are not just about her work, some of them are personal. But what is the reality? Who is Jennifer Lopez, where did she come from and how did get to where she is now? This biography aims to separate fact from fiction to reveal the real Jennifer Lopez.

OTHER BOOKS IN THE SERIES

MADONNA

Everyone thought they had Madonna figured out in early 2003. The former Material Girl had become Maternal Girl, giving up on causing controversy to look after her two children and set up home in England with husband Guy Ritchie. The former wild child had settled down and become respectable. The new Madonna would not do anything to shock the establishment anymore, she'd never do something like snogging both Britney Spears and Christina Aguilera at the MTV Video Music Awards... or would she?

Of course she would. Madonna has been constantly reinventing herself since she was a child, and her ability to shock even those who think they know better is both a tribute to her business skills and the reason behind her staying power. Only Madonna could create gossip with two of the current crop of pop princesses in August and then launch a children's book in September. In fact, only Madonna would even try.

In her 20-year career she has not just been a successful pop singer, she is also a movie star, a business woman, a stage actress, an author and a mother. Find out all about this extraordinary modern-day icon in this new compelling biography.

OTHER BOOKS IN THE SERIES

BRAD PITT

From the launch pad that was his scene stealing turn in *Thelma And Louise* as the sexual-enlightening bad boy. To his character-driven performances in dramas such as *Legends of the Fall* through to his Oscar-nominated work in *Twelve Monkeys* and the dark and razor-edged Tyler Durden in *Fight Club*, Pitt has never rested on his laurels. Or his good looks.

And the fact that his love life has garnered headlines all over the world hasn't hindered Brad Pitt's profile away from the screen either – linked by the press to many women, his relationships with the likes of Juliette Lewis and Gwyneth Paltrow. Then of course, in 2000, we had the Hollywood fairytale ending when he tied the silk knot with Jennifer Aniston.

Pitt's impressive track record as a superstar, sex symbol *and* credible actor looks set to continue as he has three films lined up for release over the next year – as Achilles in the Wolfgang Peterson-helmed Troy; Rusty Ryan in the sequel *Ocean's Twelve* and the titular Mr Smith in the thriller *Mr & Mrs Smith* alongside Angelina Jolie. Pitt's ever-growing success shows no signs of abating. Discover all about Pitt's meteoric rise from rags to riches in this riveting biography.

OTHER BOOKS IN THE SERIES

SHANE RICHIE

Few would begrudge the current success of 40-year-old Shane Richie. To get where he is today, Shane has had a rather bumpy roller coaster ride that has seen the hard working son of poor Irish immigrants endure more than his fair share of highs and lows – financially, professionally and personally.

In the space of four decades he has amused audiences at school plays, realised his childhood dream of becoming a Pontins holiday camp entertainer, experienced homelessness, beat his battle with drink, became a million-aire then lost the lot. He's worked hard and played hard.

When the producers of *EastEnders* auditioned Shane for a role in the top TV soap, they decided not to give him the part, but to create a new character especially for him. That character was Alfie Moon, manager of the Queen Vic pub, and very quickly Shane's TV alter ego has become one of the most popular soap characters in Britain. This biography is the story of a boy who had big dreams and never gave up on turning those dreams into reality.

OTHER BOOKS IN THE SERIES

JONNY WILKINSON

"There's 35 seconds to go, this is the one. It's coming back for Jonny Wilkinson. He drops for World Cup glory. It's over! He's done it! Jonny Wilkinson is England's Hero yet again..."

That memorable winning drop kick united the nation, and lead to the start of unprecedented victory celebrations throughout the land. In the split seconds it took for the ball to leave his boot and slip through the posts, Wilkinson's life was to change forever. It wasn't until three days later, when the squad flew back to Heathrow and were met with a rapturous reception, that the enormity of their win, began to sink in.

Like most overnight success stories, Wilkinson's journey has been a long and dedicated one. He spent 16 years 'in rehearsal' before achieving his finest performance, in front of a global audience of 22 million, on that rainy evening in Telstra Stadium, Sydney.

But how did this modest self-effacing 24-year-old become England's new number one son? This biography follows Jonny's journey to international stardom. Find out how he caught the rugby bug, what and who his earliest influences were and what the future holds for our latest English sporting hero.

OTHER BOOKS IN THE SERIES

ROBBIE WILLIAMS

Professionally, things can't get much better for Robbie Williams. In 2002 he signed the largest record deal in UK history when he re-signed with EMI. The following year he performed to over 1.5 million fans on his European tour, breaking all attendance records at Knebworth with three consecutive sell-out gigs.

Since going solo Robbie Williams has achieved five number one hit singles, five number one hit albums; 10 Brits and three Ivor Novello awards. When he left the highly successful boy band Take That in 1995 his future seemed far from rosy. He got off to a shaky start. His nemesis, Gary Barlow, had already recorded two number one singles and the press had virtually written Williams off. But then in December 1997, he released his Christmas single, *Angels.*

Angels re-launched his career – it remained in the Top 10 for 11 weeks. Since then Robbie has gone from strength to strength, both as a singer and a natural showman. His live videos are a testament to his performing talent and his promotional videos are works of art.

This biography tells of Williams' journey to the top – stopping off on the way to take a look at his songs, his videos, his shows, his relationships, his rows, his record deals and his demons.